CHASING MAMMON

Also by Douglas Kennedy

BEYOND THE PYRAMIDS:
TRAVELS IN EGYPT

IN GOD'S COUNTRY:
TRAVELS IN THE BIBLE BELT, USA

CHASING MAMMON

Travels in the Pursuit of Money

Douglas Kennedy

HarperCollins*Publishers*

money - History

HarperCollins*Publishers*
77-85 Fulham Palace Road,
Hammersmith, London W6 8JB

Published by HarperCollins*Publishers* 1992

9 8 7 6 5 4 3 2 1

Copyright Douglas Kennedy 1992

The Author asserts the moral right to be
regarded as the author of this work

A catalogue record for this book is
available from the British Library

ISBN 0 00 255038 5

Photoset in Linotron Bembo by
Falcon Typographic Art Ltd
Fife, Scotland

Printed in Great Britain by
HarperCollins Manufacturing Glasgow

FOR FRANK AND IRENE CARLEY
AND FOR GRACE, OF COURSE

CONTENTS

The universal regard for money is the one hopeful fact in our civilization, the one sound spot in our social conscience. Money is the most important thing in the world. It represents health, strength, honour, generosity and beauty as conspicuously as the want of it represents illness, weakness, disgrace, meanness and ugliness.

BERNARD SHAW, *Man and Superman*

AUTHOR'S NOTE

Set out to travel in pursuit of money, and you are immediately presented with a number of questions: Where should you start? What markets should you venture into? What is it about the world of the trading floor that actually intrigues you?

From the outset, I realized that I simply didn't have the economic nous required to write a conventional examination of financial markets and how they worked. I knew nothing about stocks, bonds, options or ninety-day bank bills, while acronyms like FOX, Forex, and EPS left me stupefied. And anyway, the past seven years of Big Bangs (and even bigger crashes) had produced an entire library of books on the helter-skelter world of high finance – books frequently written by former dealers who not only understood the Daedalian intricacies of the marketplace, but also had the inside dope on where the dirty linen was hidden.

There was no way that I could compete with such knowledgeable insiders. Nor did I want to. What interested me most about the marketplace was the way it illuminated attitudes towards money in a variety of cultures. I also didn't want to loiter in every major bourse on the planet, in the hope of making the definitive statement on why man chases mammon. I immediately decided to strike Tokyo off my itinerary, as I didn't feel I could add anything to the extensive analyses that already exist about the Japanese financial psyche. Similarly, in writing about Wall Street and the City of London, I decided to focus on a few individuals working within these fiscal arenas, rather than attempt a sweeping, panoramic overview. Believing that a travel book is a sort of fiction that happened – in which the narrative is shaped by the characters you meet during your perambulations – I set off with the attitude that

I was simply a layman passing through a foreign territory I'd never ventured into before. And like all my other wanderings, what would interest me most about this journey into money was the stories I picked up along the way.

As every financier will tell you, money talks. Spend some time in any financial marketplace, however, and you will discover that those who play with money also talk – and, in fact, are usually willing to talk very directly about their personal and professional lives. To travel in the realm of finance is to share in many a confidence. So, to preserve the anonymity of many of those who appear in this book, I have frequently changed names, occupations, and other personal details. The chronology of events, the whereabouts of meetings, the names of certain businesses or companies have also been tampered with. Occasionally, for the sake of the narrative, I have also amalgamated people's stories. Just as, no doubt, they amalgamated aspects of the stories they told me.

After all, in the world of the marketplace, the truth is not always the bottom line.

Some thank yous are in order.

Several companies and organizations were exceedingly helpful when it came to assisting me with transportation and/or accommodation. They include Virgin Atlantic, Qantas, Royal Air Maroc, Malev Hungarian Airlines, the Australian Tourist Commission, and the Hotel Royal Mansour in Casablanca. I would also like to thank the staff of Scott Gold-Blyth in London – and, most especially, Bronwyn Gold-Blyth – for arranging my journey to Sydney.

While on the road, hospitality and/or inside information was provided by John Iremonger, Jane Addams, Leo Guen, Iren Kiss, Laszlo Tabori, Gwen Trimble and John Hoffman. Edna Carew – Australian financial writer *extraordinaire* – not only gave me permission to steal the title for my Sydney chapter from her, but also opened up the entire world of the Sydney marketplace for me. I owe her, at the very least, a bottle of

Laphroaig. Just as I also owe several drinks to Susan Steele who painstakingly read the manuscript and, calling upon her considerable knowledge as a City financier, made certain that my financial language was up to scratch.

While tethered to my desk, I also wrote about subsidiary aspects of my travels for a variety of newspapers and magazines. Hats off, therefore, to the following editors and publications: Christine Walker at the *Sunday Times*; Dylan Jones at *Arena*; Will Ellsworth-Jones at the *Independent Magazine*; and Susan Jeffreys at the late, lamented *Listener*. Parts of Chapter 7 first appeared (in a very different form) in *GQ*. My thanks to Alexandra Shulman and Michael VerMeulen for allowing me to audition two sections of this manuscript before they appeared between hard covers.

The extract from *Man and Superman* is reproduced by permission of The Society of Authors on behalf of the Bernard Shaw Estate. The passages quoted from Alexis de Tocqueville's *Democracy in America* in Chapter One are translated by Henry Reeve (Schocken Books 1961). The lyrics on page 176 are from 'The Forecast Calls for Pain', by Walker and Plan, and are reproduced by permission of Warner Chappell Music Ltd.

CHASING MAMMON

ONE

In the Midst of Abundance

It is Christmas in New York, and I am on a train snaking its way up the Hudson, en route to visit an old college friend who earns $850,000 a year. My friend is named Ben. Like me, he is thirty-five years old. Like me, he is a by-product of upper-middle-class American life. Like me, he is married. Unlike me, he has children – four, to be exact. Unlike me, he has spent the last fourteen years of his life working on Wall Street. And unlike me, he makes big, serious money.

I haven't seen Ben since 1976. There is a very good reason for this; with the exception of the occasional hit-and-run visit to New York, I haven't spent much time in the United States during those fourteen years. But thanks to the handful of old college friends who live on the same island as I do, I have been kept informed of Ben's progress in the financial marketplace. I've heard all about his status as one of the top securities traders on the Street today. I've been told that he's a natural when it comes to dealing bonds, not to mention staying on that corporate escalator marked Up. And I'm also aware that he married a fellow classmate of ours named Sally, who was something in publishing for a while before she chose to travel down that post-feminist road of children and a life in the suburbs.

None of these details about Ben's life surprised me. What I remembered most about him from our college years was his solidity – the fact that he so obviously knew what his place in the world would be. Not that Ben ever spoke about having Wall Street ambitions. On the contrary, he was true to the spirit of the early 1970s by never publicly broadcasting his so-called game plan – though I sensed that he didn't really have one. What he did have was a character trait much admired in American life – well-roundedness. He was bright and thoughtful and reasonably erudite, but he would never hit you with his intellectual credentials. He was ambitious, he knew that 'playing to win' was a key construct of our society, yet he was also shrewd enough to realize that ambition must always be concealed behind a veneer of all-purpose bonhomie. Even in his early twenties he had possessed that blend of craggy dignity and populism which U.S. senators try to cultivate, as they know it inspires confidence. Ben also instinctively understood that a patrician naturalness was considered a virtue in a culture frequently accused of artificiality. But he never had to work hard at coming across as a 'genuine type'. His was an additive-free personality. What you saw was what you got.

With those attributes, Ben's success in American executive life was almost assured. After all, a team player with adroit political skills will always do well in a corporate culture where the 'good guy' is a highly prized species. Ben was undoubtedly a good guy, yet one who was also probably clever enough to realize that, for all its talk of teamwork – of interactive synergy – corporate life was essentially a power game. And whether he ended up playing this game in a law firm, a brokerage house or an investment bank was actually beside the point. So when I called him shortly after I arrived back in New York for Christmas, it didn't surprise me to hear him say he'd landed in the securities game by accident.

'How did I end up down here on the Street? Complete fluke, that's how. Like most things in life. Like this phone call. To what do I owe this pleasure after all these years?'

'I thought it was about time I bought you a beer again,' I said. 'Get some tips on the market . . . '

'That'll cost you two beers. What you doing Saturday afternoon?'

'Nothing much.'

'Come on up to the house then. We're having a few friends

over. Variations on Christmas party, that sort of thing. You might even recognize a face or two.'

So that's how I've ended up on this commuter train which is now sidling its way out of the city and heading for that strip of bedroom communities which adorn the banks of the Hudson. It's a grey cold smudge of a day. The sky over New York has taken on the hue of cigarette ash, and the river is a mosaic of ice. Simply looking at that glacial version of the Hudson gives me a chill, and reminds me that I'm no longer used to the extremities of a north-east American winter. Just as the terrain I'm currently crossing looks new to me, even though I passed through it so often as a kid, Ben's world – the world of the securities dealer, the corporate honcho, the six-figure salary – smacks of the familiar and the alien: familiar because it is a world for which I was, in many ways, groomed; alien because it now strikes me as an exotic territory through which I've never really travelled.

But as the train coasts to a halt, and I look up at the white clapboard townscape of the executive dormitory where Ben and his family live, I sense that this might just be a point of embarkation for a journey. A journey through that foreign territory of Big Money.

'Kennedy.'

The voice was Ben's, but the face belonged to someone else. At least, it didn't belong to the older version of Ben I had expected to see. In my mind, I had invented a quasi-Hogarthian image of Ben-as-Stockbroker: a figure of gravitas, a blocky man with thinning hair and a network of thinly etched lines around his eyes – hairline notches engraved onto his face by the '87 Crash, and by trying to cope with the financial obligations of top-income-bracket life.

The Ben who greeted me at the door didn't conform to this fleshy mental effigy. Rather, he was a perfect facsimile of the lanky, open-faced, at-ease-with-the-world undergraduate I had known fourteen years ago. His voice was as resonant and sturdy as ever; the handshake dry, muscle-bound. And, in true East Coast prep school style, he was still calling me by my last name. Even his clothes harked back to our New England college days – a crew-necked sweater, check lumberjack shirt, khaki chinos and Docksider moccasins. His home also reflected an education amidst the remnants of colonial America. It was a venerable three-storey red brick structure, fronted by a white-columned portico and furnished in early White House style. A house which – in true American patrician fashion – let it be known that the owner was a man of substance, yet one who believed that the display of money should be discreet.

'Kennedy, you're looking well.'

'You're looking even better, Ben.'

'And she's looking best of all,' said Ben, pointing to a woman who, with her Victorian print dress and chestnut brown hair braided halfway down her back, blended in perfectly with the Federalist decor.

Sally turned around. 'Welcome home, expatriate,' she said, offering me a cheek to kiss. Ben was right: despite the physical rigours of four births in half a decade, despite the mental *Sturm-und-Drang* of having a gang of under-sixes underfoot day in, day out, Sally appeared to be an unreconstructed image of her 1976 self. Looking at her was almost a form of romantic *déjà-vu*, as her long flowery dress and long plaited hair conjured up for me an entire generation of women from my student days – women who joined marches on Washington, practised organic vegetarianism, talked about their personal relationship with Eliot's 'Four Quartets', and sang 'You've Got a Friend' at parties. Women I never envisaged mothering four children in the stockbroker belt.

'Mommy!' The voice belonged to a little girl dressed in a miniature edition of Sally's countrified frock. She came barrelling across the polished wood floor and buried her head in the folds of her mother's identical dress. For a moment, it seemed as if mother and daughter had merged.

'Mommy, Nicholas hit me!'

Sally smiled at me and said, 'My daughter, Samantha. Say hello to an old friend of Mommy's, Sam.'

Sam buried her head deeper into Sally's skirts.

'Mommy! Nicholas hit me!'

'Did not!' shouted the five-year-old boy who now came sliding across the floor. He had a pageboy haircut, a white button-down shirt, and a striped school tie – the nascent preppy look.

'Did too!' Sam shouted back.

'She stole my He-Man!' Nicholas countered.

Sam was enraged. 'Did not!'

'Did too!'

'Get yourself a drink, Doug,' Sally said before stepping in to mediate this dispute.

'Glass of hot punch, Kennedy?' Ben asked, leading me into an adjoining room, where a pair of caterers were ladling warm cider and rum into cut-glass mugs. 'Think you might need one after meeting those two little charmers of ours.'

'Where are the other pair?' I asked.

'The twins? Upstairs asleep. Consuela's keeping an eye on them.'

'Consuela?'

Ben flashed me a blinding white smile. 'The Costa Rican au pair.'

'Wall Street really is treating you well.'

'So I keep trying to tell myself,' Ben said.

A balding man in a Harris tweed jacket and grey flannels sidled up to the drinks table.

'Hey, Heinemann,' Ben said. 'Look who just blew in from London. You remember Bob Heinemann, Kennedy?'

'I most certainly do,' I said, extending my hand.

'I don't believe it,' Heinemann said, pumping my outstretched mitt. 'You even look pretty much the same.'

'So do you, Bob' – though that statement was something of a lie, as Bob Heinemann's lack of hair and thick-set frame gave him a middle-aged demeanour. 'What're you doing with yourself?'

'Down on the Street, like Ben here. Meet Betty,' he said, indicating a matronly woman of around forty, wearing a severely cut grey suit with a Gucci scarf draped around her shoulders. So I met Betty, and I said hello to Bob and Betty's three-year-old daughter, Lois. Then I was slapped on the back by Ted Smollens. Back in college, Ted was noted for being the only student to wear a pair of Gucci loafers; now, he told me, he was a 'Forex guy on the Street'. He pointed to a blonde, clean-limbed woman crouching to wipe the faces of two little girls in matching print dresses.

'The wife, the kids,' Ted Smollens said.

Across the room, Sally was talking to Karen Fingerhut. Karen Fingerhut, who used to propound Marxist economic theory and collect money for the Chilean resistance movement. She had drifted into advertising copywriting after college, and had married a successful corporate attorney named Marv. Now she was telling Sally, 'You must show me your new laundry room.'

Then I got chatting with Debbie Shilts, a broker with some big investment house 'on the Street', who said that the problem with being a single woman in Manhattan could be summed up very succinctly: 'Every man over thirty is married, gay, or a psychopath.'

I downed another scoop of hot rum punch, then joined in an impromptu sing-along of 'Oh Come, All Ye Faithful' and other seasonal favourites.

Then I spent some time catching up with Howie Lowell – one-time relief worker in the Philippines, currently in Mergers and Acquisitions on the Street. Our conversation was interrupted by his wife Fran, who dragged him off to help change their infant son, Jerry – which meant that I never got a chance to ask Howie about the crucifix he was wearing on his lapel . . . though I did notice that Fran was sporting one too.

Then all of the kids in the room – and there must have been two dozen of them – were gathered together to meet some actor in a Santa Claus costume whom Ben had hired for the occasion. And as Santa ho-ho-hoed, and the kids ripped open the trinkety gifts he dispensed from a big red shoulder sack, and all the adults looked on indulgently, Sally sidled up to me and handed me yet another glass of hot rum punch.

'Great party,' I said, wondering if my words were starting to slur.

Sally surveyed the scene – her friends, their children, her husband, her kids, her house, her life. And from the glow in her eyes, I could tell that she was simultaneously moved and bemused by it all. She put her arm around my shoulder and said:

'Isn't this strange, Doug? Isn't this all very strange?'

Sally was right – it was strange. Strange because we were looking at a tableau of adult life and realizing that we were the figures in it. Strange because (as I sensed Sally was also thinking) we never expected to be part of such a vision of settled domesticity. And, for me, the scene was made even stranger by the fact that I felt professionally and financially distanced from it. I lived the manically insecure life of the freelance – moving from assignment to assignment like a habitual pick-up artist, always teetering on the fiscal tightrope, always convinced that my ultimate destiny was selling pencils in front of Harrods when the flow of commissions inevitably dried up. I didn't have investments. I didn't own shares in companies. I had never made the acquaintance of that elusive concept called 'disposable income'. And my one financial asset was a small south London flat with an Everest of a mortgage. But from what I could gauge, the incomes of my old college friends started at around $200,000 a year and climbed steadily upwards. Granted, I knew that ample monetary reward was the pay-off for a life in the realm of high finance – a world riddled with its own insecurities, its own four-in-the-morning fears. Just as I also knew that, if you found yourself making $200,000 a year, you tended to leverage yourself up to a $200,000-a-year lifestyle. Still, hearing them talk about their investments, their share options, their profit participation bonuses, their Central American au pairs, even their new laundry rooms, I couldn't help but feel like an illegal alien in a Top Income Bracket Republic.

Of course, it would have been easy for me to deride my friends' affluence. I could have dug deep into that defensive lexicon of the educated underpaid and come up with a wide variety of expressions to disparage their success. I could have called them corporate stains, or Baby Boom Babbitts, or (that perennial favourite) sell-outs. But the fact of the matter was, I didn't consider them sell-outs. Or conformists. Or smug suburbanites. Rather, my immediate impression was that they all appeared to be . . . well, grown-up. They had embraced the responsible adult world, and now exuded sense and sensibility. And it made me wonder: in America, does the getting of serious money signal the end of one's innocence? Does it turn you into a grown-up? Could this process of upper-middle-class maturation best be described by paraphrasing Corinthians:

> When I was a child, I spake as a child, I understood as a child, I thought as a child: but when I became a man I started earning in the mid-six figures, and I put away childish things.

Standing in Ben and Sally's sitting room, my brain fogged in by all that hot rum punch, the Biblical quotation flickered briefly through my head, only to be interrupted by the voice of Bob Heinemann. It was a slow, methodical voice accompanying the slow, methodical movement of his hand as he slipped one of his business cards into my breast pocket and said:

'If you don't mind coming down to Wall Street one afternoon, I'll buy you lunch.'

'How does Monday sound?' I said.

★   ★   ★

The offices of A.J. Heinemann & Co. were located in a pre-Depression skyscraper within easy jumping distance of the New York Stock Exchange. To walk into this building was to enter a still-potent symbol of 1920s American financial arrogance. Back then, an office building wasn't designed to be a high-rise concrete fortress with functional ergonomics. Instead, it was conceived as an exuberantly opulent testament to the making of money. This building's foyer certainly scored points in the opulence stakes – marble floors, gothic arches, carved figurines adorning the walls, gilded doors leading into lifts that were a reflecting chamber of black-on-silver Deco mirrors. This wasn't a house of commerce; this was a picture palace minus the mighty Wurlitzer.

Once above street level, however, the building reverted to dreary type – long corridors painted in civil-service colours, paved in scuffed linoleum, and illuminated by harsh fluorescent tubes. Fronting these corridors were office doors with frosted glass and company names embossed on them. The sort of doors behind which you'd expect to find a private eye specializing in marital infidelities. Only this being Wall Street, there were no gumshoes on the corridor – just certified public accountants, and freelance investment consultants, and small-time brokerage houses like A.J. Heinemann & Co.

There was no receptionist greeting arrivals at A.J. Heinemann & Co. No secretary either. Just a trio of motherly clerks in their fifties and a quintet of middle-aged male brokers in nondescript suits all seated at a cluster of desks in a large open-plan room. At the end of this central workspace were two glassed-in cubicles: the offices of A.J. ('Al') Heinemann and his son, Bob. Twenty-year-old furniture, calendars as wall decorations, old wooden filing cabinets, even the occasional adding machine – this was a truly antediluvian operation, with only a couple of computer terminals acknowledging the nineties. The bargain basement decor hinted that Al Heinemann was a no-frills kind of a guy who took a no-frills approach to the business of making money. I wondered whether this frugal view of mercantilism had been passed down to his son.

Bob Heinemann was on his feet as soon as I came through the door, his hand out halfway across the room as he strode towards me. He welcomed me in the same slow, almost halting voice he had used when he invited me to lunch a few days earlier. My initial impression of his prematurely middle-aged countenance was now heightened by his prematurely middle-aged suit of grey herringbone, augmented by a white button-down Brooks Brothers shirt, a subdued blue crested tie, and a grey cable-knit cardigan. No Armani togs or silk Liberty braces for Bob Heinemann. He dressed like a stockbroker from the post-war era. He dressed like his father.

'This the college guy you were telling me about?' The voice of Al Heinemann came wafting over the glass partition of his office. Immediately, Bob ushered me in.

'My dad,' Bob said. Al Heinemann gave me a chiropractic handshake. Father and son shared the same bald pate, the same small pendulum of fat under the chin, the same taste in suits. Where they parted company was in their style of talk. If Bob tended towards hesitancy in his speech, then Al was all rapid-fire repartee.

'So you went to college with Bobby, right?' Al Heinemann said.

'Right.'

'And now you live in London, right?'

'Right.'

'And Bob's gonna take you to lunch at the club?'

'Right,' Bob said.

'So have a good lunch,' Al said, grabbing his Burberry off the coat stand. 'I gotta meet a client. Jack Roth. I'll send him and Estelle your best.'

'Right,' Bob said.

'What time you back from lunch?'

'Two.'

'Right,' Al Heinemann said, and he was gone.

Bob motioned me into one of the two leatherette armchairs fronting his father's desk. Behind the desk were a
pair of picture windows which afforded a panoramic view of
New Jersey. We spent a few minutes exchanging pleasantries,
searching for a way to spark the conversation into life. It
was difficult, because at college we'd never been more than
occasional acquaintances – and ones between whom there'd
been an unspoken antipathy. I'd always had the idea that Bob
Heinemann considered me something of a major wise-ass
(which I most certainly was at the time), whereas I looked
upon him back then as a stiff, already suffering from emotional
rigor mortis at the age of nineteen. As we now searched for
common ground I could sense that we were both thinking that
this spur-of-the-moment lunch invitation had been a mistake.
Because we really had nothing to say to each other.

Still, we were stuck with each other for the next hour, so . . .
I tried to get things moving by asking Bob what he had done
immediately after college.

'Went to Mexico,' Bob said.

'Mexico? That was romantic.'

A short honk of a laugh from Bob Heinemann. 'Yeah, I
guess it was. Especially since I got a job on this ranch as a
cattle hand.'

'How'd you manage that?'

Bob glanced out the window. 'The ranch belonged to a client
of my dad's.'

'A good time down there?'

'A great time, yeah.' Another quick glance out of the
window. 'I was there till around January of 1977, after which
I toyed with the idea of going into the Peace Corps. Or maybe
doing something . . . I don't know . . . different from stockbroking. But, you know, when there's a family business . . .
well, that's something that every son in that family has to
confront. And I was the only son in our family. So, I guess, in
a way I always knew I was . . . destined to end up here. I mean,
I grew up knowing this business was here. Waiting for me.'

So Bob came back from Mexico and joined the family firm. And for the next three years he learned the basics of stockbroking before his father shipped him off to Frankfurt – 'where my dad had some business interests' – to spend six months in a brokerage house there ('Run by another friend of my dad's'). After this dash of European seasoning, Al decided his son's training was complete. He recalled Bob to Wall Street and told him he could now consider himself the heir-apparent of A.J. Heinemann & Co.

'We're a small outfit,' Bob said. 'An old-fashioned outfit with only ten employees. Investment stockbroking is our game and we handle a portfolio of around $80 million. And I think we've got a good solid business here, though I do think we're a bit weak on the marketing side, in so far that we really can't rely on referrals when it comes to generating new business. Still, we do have our loyal group of customers – though, as my dad always says, you've got to handle customers carefully. Especially since they tend to get nervous if the market starts to get shaky.'

I asked Bob if he ever got nervous about shaky markets, about taking a wrong position on a stock.

'Every stockbroker worries about the state of the market. It comes with the territory. But I never lose sleep about a position I've taken. And that's because I'm very . . . prudent about my stock positions. Just as my father and I are very prudent about the firm itself.

'You see, we'd rather remain a small company and earn a neat profit than get big and earn nothing. And that's because we both believe that stockbroking is all about risk minimization. What you can lose is greater than what you can gain, so you have to exercise caution. Caution is the keyword here.'

Bob snatched another fast peek at the world beyond the thermapane of his father's office. Then he said: 'Lunch?'

We left the building and walked down a series of narrow sidestreets, hedged in by two opposing cliffs of skyscrapers.

14

With a raw polar wind bearing down on us, negotiating this concrete crevice was like clambering across a mountain pass. Eventually we reached a large, venerable nineteenth-century mansion which appeared architecturally out of place amidst the high-rise surroundings. This was the India Club, Wall Street's oldest private watering hole for the financial community. Inside, the atmosphere was very Bostonian, very old Yankee – lots of heavy mahogany panelling, heavy oil portraits of stern nineteenth-century burghers, and heavy models of bygone naval vessels. The dining room was high-vaulted and starchily formal. A liveried waiter handed us menus and took our drinks order – Scotch for me, a Perrier for Bob, though Bob did ask for a packet of Marlboros.

'You still smoke?' I asked, silently pleased that Bob had at least one bad habit.

'Only outside of the office,' he said. 'My dad doesn't approve.'

We studied our menus. Fried fish, steak, chops, roasts – the usual stodgy club food. Around us was a landscape of pinstripes and horn-rimmed spectacles and polished black brogues: Wall Street at lunch.

'Your folks still live in the city?' Bob asked.

'Yeah, they're still holding out on the Upper West Side. How about you? Weren't you living in the East 70s for a while?'

'Up until Lois came along, Betty and I had an apartment on Lexington and 74th. But once we became parents, living in the city didn't seem viable anymore. So we moved to Connecticut.'

'Where abouts?'

'A town called Riverside.'

'Isn't that where you grew up?'

Bob turned his attention back to the menu. 'Yeah,' he said.

The drinks arrived; food was ordered. I asked Bob how he met Betty.

'We met four years ago at a party on Christmas Day – a party for Jews like us who don't celebrate Christmas.'

15

She was a self-employed businesswoman at the time, running a company that imported expensive leather goods from France and Germany. 'I always looked upon it as a small-time operation,' Bob said, 'but it was still nice that she had a little business of her own to run. Problem was, when the dollar got soft in '87, the business went belly up. You see, Betty was selling high-priced merchandise which simply couldn't be made profitable because of the volume she was dealing in. Volume is everything.'

Low volume ended Betty's business career; low volume ushered in her new role as housewife and mother. 'She got pregnant around a month after her company stopped trading,' Bob said. 'And number two is now on the way.'

I raised my glass of Scotch and offered congratulations.

'Thanks,' Bob said. 'Of course, the new baby means that the next year is going to be expensive. Just like this year was expensive, what with us moving out to the Island and Betty redecorating the house. But even with all that expenditure last year, I still managed to put a fair amount aside. I don't know about you, but when it comes to money, my financial goals are savings oriented. Especially since – the way the market is at the moment – putting money aside is a crucial concern of mine. And what we all have to realize is that our generation will never match the same standard of living that our parents had. I mean, even when you take into account salary differentials, they still had it pretty good when it came to the price of real estate or sending us to school. So, what I'm saying is, our expectations have to be different. Which is why I try to save so carefully – so I can match my parents' living standard as closely as possible.'

'And you're managing to do that?' I asked.

'Yeah, just about. But only because I follow a piece of very good advice my father once gave me: "Always live as if it was your worst year in the market."'

Lunch was served, and the conversation veered onto the subject of old college acquaintances.

'You wouldn't believe the number of people from our class who've moved to the suburbs,' Bob said. 'Granted, they're mainly up in Westchester like Ben – since Westchester is, I guess, a little cheaper to live in than Connecticut. Still, one thing you've got to say for Westchester, the commute's a bit easier. Like, Ben has got a terrific commute. Thirty minutes down the Hudson and then a ten-minute walk from Grand Central to his office. Mind you, even though I'm in Connecticut, I've got a pretty good commute too. Like I have a choice of either the 6.50 or the 7.20 to Grand Central. And since my house is only an eight-minute walk from Riverside Station, it means I can sleep till six most mornings.

'Now what's really good about those two trains is that I can always get a seat, which is not always possible on most trains after 7.30. And I find that the fifty minutes it takes me to get in to Grand Central is just about the exact length of time I need to read the *New York Times*. And then, when I get to the city, it's only a couple of stops on the subway to Wall Street. So, like I said, I can't complain commute-wise.'

'Seems like you've really got very little to complain about,' I said.

Bob ruminated on the comment for a moment or two, focusing his eyes on the plate of turkey and mashed potatoes in front of him.

'I guess I don't have much to complain about,' he finally said. 'I mean, I don't have to worry about getting fired or competing with anybody else. And, like I said, I do have a good standard of living. So, yeah, I guess my job fulfils an important consideration of mine . . . '

'What's that?'

'Making life as simple as possible.'

We lapsed into momentary silence. Bob turned his attention once again to the turkey, the mash and the reservoir of gravy they floated in. Then he looked back up at me and said:

'I really don't know why you're asking me so much about

17

myself. I mean, what I do isn't interesting. It's just an ordinary life.'

An ordinary life. Long after I parted company with Bob Heinemann outside the India Club and watched him disappear back in the direction of his office, that phrase kept rattling around my brain, nagging at me. Why did I find it so bothersome? Because the more I thought about it, the more I realized that I didn't know what an ordinary life was supposed to be. Bob Heinemann considered his to be a conventional, run-of-the-mill existence – a humdrum commute from the suburbs; a protected position in the family business; squirrelling away a solid chunk of his income every year by living in a state of perpetual fiscal caution. And my initial reaction to his litany of the mundane was predictable: Bob Heinemann, I had decided, was a man who had overdosed on embalming fluid.

But though he did have a mummified world-view, Bob Heinemann's life didn't ultimately strike me as ordinary. On the contrary, there didn't seem to be anything very ordinary about a man who pulled down $250,000 a year (Ben had supplied me with a 'ballpark figure' for Bob's annual salary). Nor was there anything terribly pedestrian about living in an upmarket suburb in Connecticut, or being the president-in-waiting of a Wall Street stockbroking firm. If anything, Bob's life could be classified as uncommon, if not privileged. All right, he may have bought into a conformist ethic. He may have chosen the soft option by playing the obedient son and following Daddy into the family business. But wasn't there something intriguing about his need to conform, to make life as simple as possible? And to downplay his obvious financial ambitions by saying that he led an ordinary life?

The more I considered my lunch with Bob Heinemann, the more I was struck by the hint of discomfiture underpinning the way he categorized his life. His ruefulness, though, didn't spring from regrets about roads not taken, or about doing what his father demanded of him. Instead, it seemed to hinge on a fear of not having enough. Bob Heinemann didn't feel entrapped by a life which he defined as mundane – rather, he feared the loss of that very mundanity; of being subjected to the capricious nature of life itself. And money had become his defensive bulwark in the struggle to keep his existence predictable, to make life as simple as possible.

The terrible irony of Bob's situation was that, despite having all the trappings of financial stability, he still exuded massive insecurity. He was convinced that he would never match his parents' standard of living, never know that inner peace bestowed on those who inhabited a state of fiscal certitude. In this sense he struck me as a Wall Street version of the Flying Dutchman, doomed perpetually to roam that commuting corridor between Connecticut and Lower Manhattan, fruitlessly searching for serenity, contentment, peace of mind. But even if he did eventually exceed his father's income, I doubted if he'd ever be satisfied, as there'd always be another barrier to climb in order to overcome his constant dread of being financially caught short. Of never having enough.

But do any of us ever have enough? Don't we all live in a state of ceaseless pecuniary yearning, always wanting more? Later that night, while rummaging through a shelf of my old schoolbooks in a back room of my parents' apartment, I happened upon a copy of Alexis de Tocqueville's *Democracy in America*. After more than 150 years, it still remains the most incisive examination of the American temperament ever written. In a section with the roll-off-the-tongue title 'Causes of the Restless Spirit of the Americans in the Midst of Their Prosperity', I came across a passage which made me sit bolt upright and marvel at its contemporary resonance:

In America I saw the freest and most enlightened men, placed in the happiest circumstances which the world affords: it seemed to me as if a cloud habitually hung upon their brow, and I thought them serious and almost sad even in their pleasures.

It is strange to see with what feverish ardour the Americans pursue their own welfare; and to watch the vague dread that constantly torments them lest they should not have chosen the shortest path which may lead to it.

A native of the United States clings to this world's goods as if he were certain never to die; and he is so hasty in grasping at all that is within his reach, that one would suppose he was constantly afraid of not living long enough to enjoy them. He clutches everything, he holds nothing fast, but soon loosens his grip to pursue fresh gratifications.

At first sight there is something surprising in this strange unrest of so many happy men, restless in the midst of abundance. The spectacle itself is however as old as the world; the novelty is to see a whole people furnish an exemplification of it.

Restless in the midst of abundance. Game, set and match to M. de Tocqueville. He may have been writing about the America of 1835, when the country was no more than a gawky adolescent, but he pinpointed a key malaise still afflicting the American psyche today. After all, every American is schooled in the notion that theirs is a majestically bountiful nation, brimming with opportunities for those willing to work for what they want (even if that means overcoming certain socio-economic handicaps along the way). No wonder the American vocabulary is peppered with expressions like 'You can be whatever you want to be', 'game plan' and 'Go for it'. No wonder the history of American popular music is riddled with big, aspirational numbers like 'My Way' and 'I Gotta be Me'. These songs and catchphrases not only reflect a philosophy of ambition, they define a world-view: a belief both in the perfectibility of man and in the ability of the individual to achieve his temporal goals through commitment and honest toil.

However, an individual (or, for that matter, a society) who

20

believes in the 'go for it' code of personal striving always faces a telling dilemma: what happens if they finally get what they're going for? Do they happily collapse into an armchair and heave a contented sigh of relief? Or do they immediately redraft their game plan and size up new goals, new needs? Once again, de Tocqueville cannily recognized that, among the Americans, this relentless pursuit of new goals was bound up with an insatiable need for material fulfilment.

> Their taste for physical gratification must be regarded as the original source of that secret inquietude which the actions of the Americans betray, and of that inconsistency of which they afford fresh examples every day. He who has set his heart exclusively upon the pursuit of worldly welfare is always in a hurry, for he has but a limited time at his disposal to reach it, to grasp it, and to enjoy it. The recollection of the brevity of life is a constant spur to him. Besides the good things which he possesses, his every instinct fancies a thousand others which death will prevent him from trying if he does not try them soon. This thought fills him with anxiety, fear and regret, and keeps his mind in ceaseless trepidation.

Had I not known that paragraph was written by a nineteenth-century French *philosophe*, I might have attributed it to a contemporary writer casting a cold eye on the American psyche during the 1980s. That decade wasn't merely a celebration of conspicuous consumption; it was also an era when self-gratification through money became an acceptable form of endeavour. Much of the reportage of the 1980s portrayed this national romance with avarice as if it were some sort of new phenomenon; as if it was the first 'Gilded Age' in American history. If anything, the eighties were largely a Technicolor update of the twenties. Consider: both decades embraced *laissez-faire* economics with a vengeance, declaring that (in the words of the pre-Depression president, Calvin Coolidge) 'the business of America is business'. Both decades put their faith in the open marketplace, looking back in scorn at the government-as-caring-uncle approach of previous eras. Given this backlash against the idea of 'mollycoddling' the weaker members of society, it's not surprising that Social Darwinism, the survival of the economically fittest, informed the ethical spirit of the two decades. Or that the real stars of both eras were the potentates of high finance. Or that style and the importance of being fabulous became the obsessions of the young, monied professional classes.

To say that America (and the rest of the developed world) discovered avarice during the 1980s is to miss the real legacy of that decade: namely, that it finally bestowed respectability on the pursuit of money for money's sake. No longer did anyone have to apologize for turning the quest for wealth and possessions into a form of self-interested crusade. No longer was a job in the financial sector considered conventional and unimaginative, and thousands of young men and women made a dash for the world's financial centres to test their mettle and stamina in the arenas of Pure Money. For money – as dozens of glossy magazine features reminded us – was the New Sex. Indeed, the focus on money-as-personal-fulfilment sharpened as people realized that a casual act of physical love could now be lethal.

In the eighties, life in the bourses of the world was depicted as a life-or-death struggle engaged in by new-fangled gladiators. The standard uniform for this warrior class was the power suit (of both the male and female variety), sometimes augmented by such flamboyant symbols of prosperity as red silk braces and Rolex watches. The principal weapons used in these colosseums were the telephone and the computer terminal, along with a formidable set of vocal chords, as the ability to shout down your fellow combatants during the height of conflict apparently counted for much.

But every time I watched television footage of a financial

market at full, high-decibel throttle, I found myself wondering: what are these people really shouting about? What elusive goal are they chasing? What is driving them on?

Greed, maybe? That was the kneejerk response. Greed, we were told, was good for us. It sharpened our predatory instincts and made us push ourselves beyond conventional boundaries into new frontiers. Greed – according to the boom logic of the eighties – begot 'creative thinking'. It was a force for change. And it rewarded us with . . . things.

Things. What sort of things? Designer accommodation, designer clothes, designer wheels? Is that what all that cardiac-inducing behaviour on the floor of an exchange was for? Perhaps. But as a City stockbroker friend once told me (after imbibing nearly half a bottle of Highland malt):

'I spent years wanting a company Jaguar, and fretting about the fact that my employers kept giving me a Golf GTi. It didn't matter that the GTi was a top-of-the-range convertible and about 16k worth of automobile. I had to have a Jag. Because I thought a Jag would prove my true worth as a dealer; would prove that I had finally joined the Big Boys. So I spent a solid year putting in fourteen-hour days to double my profit performance for the firm. In order, of course, to get that Jag. Which I finally succeeded in doing. They even let me choose the model I wanted – an XJS convertible, with a price tag of 38k. But you know what really got to me? The first day I was driving the car, I thought to myself – "Okay, I've got the Jag. Now what?"'

I couldn't have invented a better parable for the 1980s. Yet this stockbrokerly confession didn't strike me as an acknowledgment of greed. Instead, there was something curiously poignant about my friend's story. Just as there was also something strangely affecting about Bob Heinemann's need to match his parents' standard of living. And though I knew that these were just two isolated examples, they still served as reminders that the pursuit of money didn't always dovetail neatly with the pursuit of avarice; that simply to categorize the marketplaces of the world as theatres of greed was to commit a gross oversimplification.

The quest for money, after all, is bound up in the quest for personal validation. Money is an essential component of the way we define our lives to ourselves and to others. It is, therefore, a continual source of personal tension, as its presence shadows our every move. We spend the bulk of our lives scrambling after the folding stuff, hoping it will give our time on the planet some value, some import. For these reasons, money is often worshipped. Yet, like any questionable deity, there is a tricky underside to its sorcery – no matter how much money we have, we are never completely satisfied.

Could it be that we constantly want more money because we constantly need to reassure ourselves that we have a reason for being here? And if that is the case, does money provide our lives with a tragic subtext – a realization that we will *never* have enough; that we will always be restless in the midst of abundance?

Much of the 1980s may have been a dance in praise of Mammon, but don't believe for a moment that that dance has suddenly been deemed *outré* in the eco-conscious, good Samaritan nineties. As de Tocqueville noted, the disquieting effect of money upon mankind is a spectacle as old as the world itself. We may have said goodbye to a decade of glitzy cupidity, but the issue of money and how we use it to justify our existence is still with us. Just as it has always been with us.

If there is one lasting legacy of the Roaring Eighties, it is this: we have now come to look upon money as a global commodity, and one which moves around the planet at the speed of light. Consider: a bad news blip on a Reuters screen in a Tokyo trading room will spend the day following the sun, causing seismic repercussions as brokers turn on their terminals in Singapore, Bahrain, Frankfurt, London, New York, Chicago, Los Angeles and Sydney. Thanks to an umbilical cord of microchips and satellite communications, the world's financial markets have now become inexorably linked to one another. Like members of a manic encounter group, they are dependent upon each other for their mutual equilibrium.

Just because world markets are electronically interconnected, however, doesn't mean that the players operating in these pecuniary hippodromes share similar ideas about money. Though they may all be dealing with the same chunk of capital, their notions about the uses of that capital – what money means to them – are bound to be radically different. Perceptions of money are as diverse as national cultures themselves. So it struck me that, by spending some time lingering in a handful of major and minor financial centres around the world, not only might I discover wildly disparate attitudes towards money and its applications in various societies, I would also be afforded a window on those societies. For a financial market is the obvious sphere of action in which to explore the pursuit of money, as it deals with money in its purest, most abstract state – as a dancing number on a screen. As a commodity unto itself.

What interested me, most was not how these markets worked; rather, what made people work in them? And what, in turn, did that tell us about the internal temperament of a culture, a nation? As someone who didn't speak the *lingua franca* of high finance, I knew that I would be an innocent abroad in these realms of money. I also knew that to try and cover every big-league stock exchange in the world would be ultimately befuddling. Anyway, I didn't want my travels to have a fixed market-to-market itinerary. Like all of my previous journeys, I'd let happenstance (and the people I met 'on the road') point me in the direction of my next destination.

After all, happenstance had led me to that party at Ben's, and to that subsequent lunch with Bob Heinemann. Just as, later that night, happenstance led me to that volume of de Tocqueville, and to the discovery that I had half a dozen business cards tucked into the breast pocket of the jacket I was wearing. They were the calling cards of all those college contemporaries I'd met again at Ben's. When I laid the cards out on my bed – like someone playing a makeshift game of solitaire – I saw that they all worked in and around Wall Street.

Looking at those business cards was like looking at a collection of prospective entry visas. And the next morning, I started making some phone calls to see if these thirty-five-year-old financiers would let an old acquaintance into their world for a while.

Three Tales of Innocence
and Experience

It was one of those restaurants where the menu read like
a primer in aesthetics, and where the food appeared to be
travelling under a series of assumed names. A collection of
salad greens arrived, calling itself hydroponic lettuce with
crème fraîche and dill. The monkfish showed up incognito
under a nutmeg and juniper berry glaze, embellished with
organic mangetout. Even the lemon sorbet was using the
alias of citron frappé steeped in Stolichnaya. Eating here
was like being cast in the role of an immigration officer
at a contentious border post, and coming to the conclusion that every identity was suspect; that everything presented to you was a heavily disguised version of something
else.

Toby told me it was his favourite restaurant in Manhattan.
He liked the *nouvelle americaine* cuisine. He liked the reduc-
tionist decor – the distressed walls, the tubular steel furniture,
the hi-tech pendulums of light overhanging every table. He
even liked the waiters – all dressed in minimalist black,
all fluent in Chic Foodspeak. Ours was called Calvin, and
he persuaded Toby to order a $30 bottle of Californian
chardonnay 'because of its oaky atmospherics'. Toby said
that he approved of a chardonnay with 'a woody subtext',
but he said it in a hesitant, eager-to-please sort of way,
as if he wanted the waiter's approval for his cosmopolitan
credentials. As if he wanted to deny the fact that he was
Tobias Wong, a third-generation Malaysian-American from
Indianapolis, Indiana – where nouvelle cuisine meant ordering

a salad at Burger King; where 'oaky atmospherics' conjured up images of a Boy Scout campfire.

Tobias Wong. I'd always liked the incongruity of that name. It's a splendid example of the sort of quirky ethnic counterpoint that is so intrinsically American. Just as Toby himself was an embodiment of a particularly Malaysian-American contradiction, as he had his parents' Asian features coupled with a flat, unvarying voice that conjured up the flat, unvarying topography of the American midwest. Which was, after all, his home turf.

Tobias Wong. Yet another passing acquaintance from my college years. I remembered him as exuding an inoffensiveness which obviously masked a personality of substantial intricacy. He always dressed in studiously inoffensive college-boy clothes – Oxford cloth shirts, neatly pressed denims, a heavy blue down parka to insulate him against the New England winter. Fourteen years on, he was still dressing in a studiously inoffensive way – updated versions of the same yellow button-down shirt, the same sharply creased Wranglers, the same blue parka. For someone trying to assume the identity of a Manhattan sophisticate, his choice of clothes was decidedly homespun. But there was something oddly affecting about his lack of stylishness, and the way it negated his attempts at urbanity. It suggested yet again that Toby was trying to straddle several worlds at once; that contradiction was his natural habitat.

'Funny running into you at Ben's party,' Toby said after Calvin had gone off in search of our wood-cured chardonnay. 'I mean, you were about the last person I expected to see there.'

'I've been away a long time.'

'London okay?'

'London's very okay. How's New York treating you?'

'That's something of a long story,' Toby said in a let's-not-get-into-that-right-away tone. I took the hint, and redirected the conversation into more neutral waters. For the next forty-five minutes or so – in the course of which Calvin smoothly hustled us through three courses and the bottle of wine (thereby maintaining the 'fed-watered-and-out-in-an-hour' timetable which most fashionable New York restaurants must adhere to) – we played the 'Whatever happened to . . .' game. This is a game in which a pair of old friends pick through the debris of other acquaintances' lives, and thus avoid having to talk immediately about their own circumstances. It also gives the participants the chance to weigh up their successes and failures in the light of the perceived successes and failures of people they knew in that insouciant period before they had to earn a living.

Toby and I turned out to be exceedingly adroit players of the game. Especially since we both silently understood that the basic point of the exercise was to remind ourselves of the way undergraduate promise and ambition are tempered or mutated by the realities of adult life. The fact that we were also able to settle an old score or two in the process – and to do so in voices of specious concern – added a sardonic undertone to the proceedings.

When Toby mentioned a star biochemist in our class named Jake Kleinmann who abandoned pure science after college and had gone on to corner the adolescent acne market as a dermatologist in Cleveland, I remembered that Toby had also entered college wanting to be a biochemist. But whereas Jake had shown an Alexander Fleming-esque talent for bacteriology, Toby failed his first-term biochem finals – which led him to abandon the realm of pure science and choose economics as an alternative subject. That, in turn, pointed him in the direction of Wall Street after he got his degree. Which was the principal reason we were having dinner tonight.

'You're not rushing off anywhere now, are you?' he said, after calling for the bill.

'No plans at all.'

'Then come on over to the apartment. Stephanie and the baby are up at her parents' for the weekend. It'll be easier to schmooze there than in this place.'

Schmooze. Pure New Yorkeze. Spoken by a man who

29

was obviously intimidated by a restaurant which, with its *beau monde* affectations, was also pure New Yorkeze. Toby, I decided, really was a stranger in a strange land.

We handed over an immense sum of money to Calvin and made for the door.

'Liked the food, hated the bill,' Toby said *sotto voce* as we struggled into our coats.

'Then why eat here?'

'Because it's New York, isn't it?'

We hit the street. It was one of those raw sub-arctic nights when you could almost believe that Manhattan was twinned with Irkutsk. Toby's apartment was only a few blocks away from the restaurant, but our dash from Third Avenue to York was like a winter reconnaissance mission across frozen tundra, as the pavements were a skating rink of ice and the mercury had dive-bombed to frostbite territory. By the time we reached his building my feet had been rendered senseless, and as we crossed the centrally-heated threshold of his apartment I was hoping that a whisky might be proffered to assist the thawing process. But Toby (as if reading my mind) said that all he had in the way of liquid antifreeze was herbal tea or decaf. So I made do with a cup of emasculated coffee.

Toby's was a standard-issue Upper East Side apartment. Two small bedrooms, a galley kitchen, parquet floors, white walls, eight-foot ceilings. We sat in the corner of an oblong living room, on a pair of matching sofas with generic chintz covers. Two matching teak veneer side tables were crammed with framed family snaps of Toby and Stephanie (a banker with Chase Manhattan, and the sort of heavily scrubbed American woman who wears cashmere and pearls and tartan skirts adorned with large bobby-pins) and their two-year-old daughter Sophie. The furniture had a certain anti-Manhattan bias to it, as if it had been bought with the inevitable move to the suburbs in mind. So it didn't surprise me when Toby said they were thinking of 'relocating' to Westchester County sometime next year.

'The city's been . . . well, fun, I guess, most of the time.
But, you know, I've had my urban experience. And with a
baby, it's sort of time to . . . well, you know, make that move
to somewhere more . . . settled. Especially since I'm working
in software now.'

'Software?' I said. 'I thought you were still down on Wall
Street.'

'I was. Up until last month.'

'What happened?'

Tobias smiled an awkward, hesitant smile. 'I got fired.'

'Shit, Toby . . . '

'No need for sympathy. I mean, I'm kind of used to getting
fired by now. Since this is the third time it's happened to me
in eighteen months.'

There was an awkward silence followed by another awkward, hesitant smile from Toby. 'It's been what I guess you
could call an interesting year and a half,' he said. 'And you
know, the funny thing is, when I ask myself, "Why has this
all been happening to me?" . . . when I look for some sort of
conceptual linkage to explain this series of career glitches . . .
you know what I come up with? That biochem course I failed
in my first year at college, which basically ended my hopes of
being a research chemist.'

I said that failing an introductory course surely didn't have
to mean an end to his career in science.

'I blew a theoretical math course the next semester as well,'
he said. 'And with two Fs on my transcript, there was no way
I'd ever get accepted at a graduate school for a master's or
doctorate in chemistry. Which meant there was also no way
I'd ever get a chemistry-related job. It was a bit of a shock to
discover, at the age of eighteen, that I wasn't going to be what
I always thought I'd be. Like, my father's a chemist, and my
grandfather was a chemist, so I guess I thought that would be
my destiny too.'

The discovery that he could actually fail at something had
sent Toby into a funk for several months, as the statement

'I've failed' is just about the most dreaded admission one can make in American life (many would argue it's even worse than announcing: 'I have a terminal illness'). But during his second year at college, Toby decided to put failure behind him and reinvent his future. He had hit upon a new 'career option' – he was going to be a sportswriter. He'd always been something of a fanatic about football, so he started writing about local games for the college newspaper, and soon reached the conclusion that a life spent commenting upon the gladiatorial rites of an American autumn would be very sweet indeed.

That is, until he heard about the money involved in sportswriting. He was down in Boston, covering a college football game, and he got talking to a staff journalist from the *Boston Globe* sitting next to him in the press box. When Toby mentioned that he was considering going professional as a sportswriter after college, the hack laughed cheerlessly and said, 'Well kid, gotta tell you – it's a great life. A really great life. As long as you don't mind driving a nine-year-old car when you're pushing forty, and living in a shit suburb, and never having any money to go anywhere, and thinking that a dinner out at your local Eyetie dump is a big splurge – 'cause that's all you're gonna be able to afford, since you'll only be pulling down twelve grand a year. So, like I said, sportswriting's a real great career. Just remember to take a vow of poverty before you land your first job.'

Twelve grand a year at the age of forty? Toby had friends who'd just left college and were already earning twelve grand a year on executive training programmes at various banks. Suddenly sportswriting lost its romantic allure, and Toby decided to 'get practical' again. He took an economics course.

'From the moment I sat through my first introductory economics class, I knew that this was for me. There was a logic and a structure to it, but it wasn't theoretical. And I started getting really idealistic about how I might be able to apply economics when it came to helping people. I know that sounds kind of lame, talking about wanting to help people, but

I really believed that I could do some good back then. Which is why I spent my junior year in Kuala Lumpur – because I was planning to specialize in developmental economics, and because Kuala Lumpur was kind of my ancestral home. So I thought, why not put my economic education to work for my own people? And when I got back to the States that May, I landed a summer job with the Asian Division of the First National Bank of Boston, which was great. Real great. So great that I started thinking about maybe going to graduate school, maybe getting a degree in Asian economics before heading out to K.L. again.'

Toby never got that advanced degree, nor did he ever venture back to the island of his forefathers. Instead, he 'got practical' once again. As soon as he received his undergraduate diploma, he found a place in a major bank's executive training programme. All right, it wasn't 'helping people' kind of work, nor did it have the techno-exotic allure of Far East economics. But it was run according to 'organizational systems in keeping with the bank's hierarchical multinational design'. Toby found this corporate-speak very reassuring, as it hinted that he would be entering an intensely structured world. And he craved structure because he feared that, without it, the wilful, undisciplined side of his personality would assert itself. Entering into a company structure, he believed, would keep his more capricious, headstrong tendencies in check. It would erect a *cordon sanitaire* around that part of himself he'd always kept hidden from public view.

'Now, at first the training programme was terrific. Just terrific. Especially since it was in the Commercial Lending Division of the bank. And that's where I wanted to be, since what we were being trained to do was sell loans for the bank, and I kind of liked the idea of being a high-powered salesman, convincing businesses and governments to borrow money from us. And I was doing well. Real well. Or at least that's what I thought. But then, around four months into the programme, one of the bank's senior vice-presidents took me aside and said: "Toby, we've identified you as a superior problem solver with great analytical skills. But when it comes to the politics of corporate life – of business itself – well, you've still got some growing up to do. You're just too informal, too much of a loose cannon to work in a people-sensitive area like commercial lending. So we've decided to transfer you into Operations for a while."

'Well, I've got to tell you, I was crushed by this news. Especially since I thought I was a team player. I was the only one on the training programme who didn't stay in Commercial Lending. And Operations had this reputation for being a one-way ticket to nowhere. It was so b-o-r-i-n-g – what you're dealing with in Operations is real lively stuff like bank statements and the smooth operation of cash machines. I mean, I was young and bright and full of ideas, but I was in a dead-end division surrounded by dead wood. Dead wood who wanted to keep me down. So I called up the personnel officer of the Liability Management section of the bank and asked for a transfer.'

That was a mistake. According to the rigorous structure of corporate life, Toby had tried to buck the bank's hierarchical executive system – which, in the eyes of the bank's hierarchical management, was something akin to an act of heresy. Toby's boss, the executive vice-president of Operations, hauled him into his office and said: 'Toby, did you really call up Liability Management and ask for a transfer?'

'I hate my job.'

'You may hate your job, but you didn't follow the operative procedure for letting us know that you hate your job. You have to keep to procedure around here.'

After this, Toby was branded a 'non-team player' – which, in corporate-speak, was the equivalent of being called a Red in the McCarthy era. Worse still, Operations became a kind of gulag to him – a punishment camp to which he had been sentenced for an indefinite term. He was not a model prisoner. Whenever he put in a twelve-hour day (which was frequently), he would come in an hour later the following morning – in direct contravention of 'operative procedure'. Once, when an immediate superior ordered him not to wear Reeboks around the office (they were considered bad for the corporate image), Toby told him that nobody – repeat, nobody – gave him orders. Especially when he was still only making seventeen grand a year.

Eventually, it was suggested to Toby by the personnel director that he might prefer 'a less structured corporate environment'. In plain English, this meant 'Hit the road, Jack.' So he did, learning how to deal bonds for a big multinational investment bank down on the Street.

'Do you know what the difference is between a bond and a bond trader?' Toby asked. 'A bond matures faster.

'That was a real mistake, switching into the bond game. 'Cause it was peopled by assholes who actually believed they were doing something of consequence by screaming all day. And I'll be quite honest: I just couldn't deal with the whole cut-and-thrust of the bond game. I didn't have the acumen required to be a dealer. So I was almost relieved when they let me go. It helped that they softened the blow by telling me I was simply a victim of a whole big corporate restructuring they were doing at the time. But I knew the truth, of course: I couldn't cut it on the market floor.'

Toby couldn't cut it either at his next port of call, a financial house where his job was to drum up customers for the Equity Division. In his first five months, he managed to bring in one minor-league client. In his sixth month, he was told that his services would no longer be required.

'The day I got my notice, I called up Stephanie at the bank where she works and said, "Honey, we got the double play." I knew my Wall Street career was over. And I was kind of relieved, because I finally realized that I never wanted to be there in the first place.'

But, with his share of a New York mortgage to pay, Toby still had to find a job. He fell back on a few subsidiary computer skills he'd picked up over the years, and now he was working for a company which installed software in financial houses around the city.

'Bet you think that sounds like a seriously boring job,' he said. 'Well, it is boring, but at least it's reasonably well remunerated, so I can't complain. Like, I know this is only temporary. I went to see a psychic recently, and she told me that I was an architect when it came to recognizing patterns of energy, and that this was a period of transitional energy for me.

'So what I'm really working on now is a personal project I've labelled "Internal Revamp". Building from the inside out. And the first positive move I've taken is to get out of the city next month, because the energy here just isn't working out for me, and Stephanie has been very worried about my professional instability, and thinks a more soothing residential environment would help. So we're renting a place in New Rochelle, around forty minutes north of Manhattan. Stephanie will keep commuting into the city, but my company has agreed to let me work around Westchester County, where the alpha waves are a lot less stressful. And once we're settled up in New Rochelle, I'm going back to school.'

'What are you planning to study?' I asked.

'Shamanistic healing.'

Tobias Wong – thwarted chemist, thwarted sportswriter, thwarted Third World economist, thwarted financier . . . and now, shamanistic healer? To many, his curriculum vitae would have seemed like that of a perennial loser. To me, however, he was simply someone who had fallen into the very common American trap of choosing a profession on the basis of pay rather than desire. Listening to him, I couldn't help but think of the many times during my student days when I too was warned about going into something absurdly insecure like the theatre or the writing game. 'Get a law degree,' I was always advised by my father, who – though a corporate man himself – so obviously hated the internecine stupidity of corporate life.

His rationale was that law would 'always give you something to fall back on'. But the way I figured it, by the time I had the law degree and was in a job, I'd be used to living a metropolitan life on a lawyer's salary, which meant that I'd find it desperately hard to get off the $100,000 a year corporate wage-slave treadmill. Anyway, the idea of being a lawyer was about as alien to me as joining a Benedictine order, but I still pondered the notion very carefully. Although we like to brag about our rugged individuality, the educated American middle classes are, at heart, raised to embrace the corporate ideal, and urged to keep their professional sights carefully focused on conventional, well-remunerated vistas.

Given his loose-cannon idiosyncrasies, Toby was obviously a non-starter in the competitive good-guydom of corporate life. Yet fear of the financial unknown – fear of having to make do on twelve grand a year if he pursued his sportswriter fantasy – plunged him into a professional cul-de-sac of his own making. Only now, as he confronted his late thirties, was he trying to find his way out. Yet, as we sipped our low-octane coffee and he told me about his future plans in altered-state healing, I couldn't help but feel strangely optimistic about Toby and his future.

After all, how many failed investment bankers get the chance to transform themselves into the future Shaman of New Rochelle?

She always had a small rucksack slung over her shoulder, and a red bandana dangling out of the pocket of her denims. She always used salutations like 'Hey, guys!' and actually said 'neat' when something met her approval. When I first encountered her in 1972, she struck me as the suburban archetype whom my mother would have approvingly dubbed 'a nice girl'. But I never liked nice girls back then (I had a romantic penchant for willowy cellists or wholesale neurotics who mainlined Sylvia Plath), so I wrote Debbie Shilts off as the perennial good sport: pert, yet enthusiastically *ordinaire*.

It was, of course, a harsh assessment, and one which I immediately amended when I heard that, shortly after we got our degrees, Debbie had disappeared to Cameroon with the Peace Corps. Nice girls from New Jersey generally didn't spend two years of their lives teaching English in a tumbledown village on the outskirts of Douala, so the news genuinely intrigued me at the time. But, since Debbie and I didn't keep in touch, the first time I had a chance to ask her why she'd ventured to Cameroon was fourteen years later, at Ben's party.

'You want to hear the story, come on down to the Street,' she said.

So I did just that, dropping by her office near the Stock Exchange a week later. Debbie worked on the fourteenth floor of one of those anonymous glass and concrete cubes that spread like architectural body lice across the Manhattan cityscape during the sixties. Her office was a small cell-like cubicle constructed out of pre-fab soundproof dividers. It afforded a panoramic view of an air shaft. A slot-in nameplate adorned the door of this and the thirty-two other cubicles stacked back-to-back down a narrow corridor. Each cubicle was furnished with the same wood and steel desk, the same hi-back swivel chair in black fabric, the same grey filing cabinet, the same Apple Macintosh computer. This was the investment brokerage section of a major financial corporation. Debbie had evidently been inducted into its Order of Shoulder Pads, as she was crisply dressed in a navy blue suit and white linen blouse, a blue silk bow neatly adorning its collar. The nice girl in a power corporate uniform.

'Cameroon must seem far away from all this,' I said, settling into the client chair facing her desk.

'Well, it was twelve years ago,' she said. 'But, yeah, it does kind of belong to another time – to the point where it's really like ancient history to me. And whenever I get thinking about those two years, you know what always comes to mind? The light. I could never get over its harshness. That's the thing which haunts me most about Africa – remembering just how pure the sun was; how it made everything so clear.'

'Unlike the light in New York?'

Debbie pointed to the air shaft beyond her window. 'What light?

'You know, before I got to Cameroon, I had these real stupid visions of Africa being Tarzan-ish. But where I was – this little village around fifty miles from the capital – really reminded me of being in a more primitive version of Alabama. You know, the real backwoods South with sharecropper shacks and stuff. And I was living in this hut with no running water or electricity, so it was kind of like spending two years in this real remote summer camp. And I'd often wake up in the mornings and ask myself, "What am I doing here?"'

'Well, what were you doing there?'

Debbie said that being despatched to the environs of Douala had been the stuff of fluke. A month or two before she got her degree, she was browsing through that corner of the college reference library which was set aside for 'Career Options' brochures. Beneath a pile of papers extolling a future in actuarial science, she unearthed a Peace Corps application form. It was 1976 – a recessionary time. The job market had contracted, and Debbie was a little uncertain about what to do with a B.A. in English. What's more, she'd never been beyond the frontiers of her native land, so the discovery of that Peace Corps application led to romantic visions of doing good deeds in designer khakis under a hot tropical sun.

'I filled in the form, sent it off and went for an interview. A month later, I got a phone call: could I leave for Douala in three weeks' time? I thought: what have I got to lose? And that was the next two years of my life accounted for.'

'Accounting for' the way she used her time was important to Debbie. So important that, after two relatively heedless years in Cameroon, she declined the opportunity to travel for a few months after her Peace Corps stint was over and flew straight home into a teacher training course at New York University.

A year later, she slotted into a job as an instructor in English at a community college in a thoroughly unsalubrious corner of the Bronx.

'Now that I think about it, the five years I spent teaching at that college were deeply insane . . . and quite wonderful. I mean, I was taking the subway uptown every morning into this hellhole of a neighbourhood, trying to teach American literature to people whose first language was usually Spanish. And the pay was buttons – twenty-three grand a year. Starvation money in New York. But I still somehow managed on it. Like, I was living in this tiny $250 a month room in a residential hotel on 108th and Broadway – a real dump. I never spent money on clothes or eating out, and since most of my friends in the city were other teachers at the college, I had no real sense of missing out on that upscale side of New York life. Up until two months before I quit, I really thought I'd be a teacher for the rest of my life.'

What brought about this sudden departure from Bronx academic life? Shortly after her thirtieth birthday, the college's Dean of Faculty informed Debbie that, with great regret, she was being denied tenure. City cutbacks had blocked her promotion, and she essentially had a year to find herself a new job.

'Like I said earlier, I'm a pretty programmed sort of person. So when I was told that I was out on my can from the college, I immediately looked for something else to programme into. And, you know, passing the big three-O got me thinking about where I was going and whether I really wanted to keep on living in that creepy hotel. It was 1985 and the whole money thing was starting to become important. And then I went to a high-school reunion back in Jersey, and ran into one of my oldest girlfriends, who was now some big corporate lawyer in Washington. You know what she said when we met? "Well, I'm glad to see one of us is still wearing dungarees and long hair." Some other guy there said the same sort of thing: "Still carrying a backpack, Debbie?"

'I was being perceived as some kind of throwback to the sixties, some kind of anachronism. And I guess it really got to me, 'cause I date my whole growing awareness of money to around that time. Another thing was, I was boyfriendless back then. I just wasn't meeting eligible guys being a teacher up in the Bronx. And I started thinking: there's no way you're going to attract a man in the mid-1980s by living in a residential hotel and dressing like you're still en route to Woodstock.'

Debbie decided she needed to programme into a more lucrative future. She tried data processing for a while, but discovered that it was the equivalent of being on novocaine from nine to five every workday. Then a friend told her about the wonderful world of brokerage sales – working in a major financial house as a sort of investment doctor for individual clients, helping them make the most of their money. She signed on for a training programme, and within a few weeks she decided that it was her destiny.

What she immediately liked about the business was the fact that it gave you individual autonomy; you were put in the position of a salesman who had to hustle for clients. You were paid a very basic salary, and you made your real money on commission.

'The brokerage house I work for has a basic policy towards people like me: as long as I bring money into the company, don't cost the company anything, and make certain I don't do something illegal that would bring the Securities and Exchange Commission into the office, they leave me alone. So, on the asset side, I've got the corporate structure behind me without having to put up with all that corporate in-fighting. On the deficit side, my income is all down to how much business I pull in. And, at the start, it was a real bitch to find clients. I mean, in my first year I only made $19,000 gross – four grand less than what I was pulling in as a teacher. The next year I inched it up to $23,000. The year after that, $35,000. And then, finally, the dyke broke in my third year, and I've been grossing around seventy grand since then.

'But, y'know, seventy grand is not big money. Like, there are sixty brokers in my division of the company, all out there hustling for biz, and I'm ranked twenty-sixth in the pay stakes. A real mid-ranking, as far as I'm concerned. To make it worse, I got myself into really heavy debt during the first three years I was in the business.'

How did Debbie manage to slip into the red? Simple: when she first got the job at the investment house, she decided that, even if she wasn't earning an executive salary as yet, she'd still have to start living like a successful investments broker. So she moved out of the *vie bohème* furnished hotel room and laid down a $2500 deposit on a $1250 a month one-bedroom apartment on Second Avenue in the East 70s. Little things like tables and chairs and a bed meant another $2200 in outlay. Then there was the matter of business clothes: another $1200 dropped at Lord & Taylor and Bergdorf Goodman on the basics: three suits, half a dozen blouses, four new pairs of shoes ('And I bought quality, because I wanted to look quality'). But even after taking out a $5000 loan to cover this initial 'lifestyle investment' in upward mobility, Debbie still had to borrow another $15,000 over the next two years to cover all the restaurant-hopping and general executive networking that went with the territory of being a seemingly successful investments broker.

Even now, pulling down a very respectable $70,000 a year, Debbie found that she was only just coping – especially since the $300 a month rent increase on her apartment and the interest on her loans were soaking up any potential disposable income. Then there were such necessities of life as her $5000 share of a two-month summer rental in the Hamptons, and the $2000 she'd just smacked down to join a midtown Manhattan tennis club.

'I really hate admitting this, but the only reason I took the house in the Hamptons and joined the tennis club was to meet guys. And, y'know, whenever I start getting depressive about work and stuff, I start thinking just how much I bought into

42

that whole eighties culture, and how I believed that being a broker would make me seem so much more interesting. But now I realize I was trying to make myself more attractive. Like, I'd been alone a long time. Never had a boyfriend in the Peace Corps. Never had a boyfriend when I was teaching. I only had . . . events – and usually with losers. But, as I told you at Ben's party, the shortage of available men in this city is chronic. So, I guess, I had this dumb idea that going down to the Street would inevitably mean meeting an available broker with a six-figure income.'

But no pinstriped hunk ever appeared on the work front, or even on the sandy dunes of the Hamptons or in a game of mixed doubles. Instead, Ronald fell into her life.

She happened upon him, in time-honoured New York tradition, at that renowned pick-up spot for the city's educated unattached: the Museum of Modern Art. In the past, the area in front of Picasso's *Guernica* was a favourite hunting ground for single people with Knut Hamsun novels tucked under their arms. But since its repatriation to the Prado in Madrid, the action has switched to Jackson Pollock's *Number One* – one of his massive 'action paintings'; a splatter canvas which affords two strangers numerous conversational openers along the lines of: 'Don't you think Pollock's entire *Weltanschauung* was rooted in the apocalyptic post-Hiroshima world order?'

When Debbie met Ronald in front of that Pollock, however, no such aesthetic pseud-talk escaped their lips. Instead, she took the initiative by asking him about the collection of Raymond Carver stories which was protruding from the pocket of his corduroy jacket. This led them to having a coffee together in the museum café, which in turn led them to having dinner together the following weekend, and sleeping together later that night. The involvement was still in progress a full three months after that first modern art encounter. Given Debbie's past history, three months ranked as a major long-term relationship. Was she in love? She hesitated before answering.

'Ronald is the most caring, gentle man I have ever met.'

In other words, Ronald was not exactly Debbie's romantic ideal. There were two basic reasons for this: one, he was fifty-two years old, and two, he was a teacher.

In fact, he was an art teacher at a Quaker day school in Brooklyn – an ageing BoHo totally out of tune with the spirit of the times. He lived in one large room in a bleak industrial corner of Flatbush. He scraped by on eighteen grand a year. His idea of eating out was a pastrami on rye at his local kosher deli. His idea of power dressing was wearing a tie. Having eschewed the genteel frugality of teaching in favour of the supposed material glamour of brokerage sales, Debbie now found herself entangled with someone who still used empty chianti bottles to make lamps.

'A lot of single women I know who work on the Street tend to be incredibly tough and defensive – because that's what being a woman on your own in the New York financial world does to you. So I really am grateful to Ronald for giving me a necessary emotional base, a sense of equilibrium. I just wish he was younger and making more money.

'It's a real stumbling block, the money thing. Like, I'm sure this sounds ultra-tacky, but I still dream of being involved with someone who's making at least as much as me. I mean, I was brought up to believe that a man would ultimately take care of me. But by the time I reached college, the whole feminism thing came along and we were told that we shouldn't rely on men for anything. And then, the whole puffed-up confidence of the eighties made everyone believe that fulfilling your potential was all about making money – and that emotional fulfilment was also, in part, about finding someone who was making big bucks too.

'But now . . . now I don't really know who I should be, or what I should want. Like, every time I decide to slot into a new life programme, everything around me changes. The way things are going now, I'm sure that teaching's going to be considered a real prestige profession in five years' time. I'm starting to think that my career timing is shit.'

I asked Debbie what, if anything, would make her happy right now.

'Wiping out that $20,000 debt would really thrill me. Biggest mistake I ever made – borrowing money to finance a new life. Because now I'm tethered to that new life until the debt's paid off. And y'know what really gets me? The fact that I got myself into debt in order to conform – to hang up my backpack and be like every other jerk in a suit. But I guess I wanted to be like everyone else of my generation when it came to having money – and now it's costing me.

'In fact, it's costing me $400 a month for the next five years.'

On the day after Christmas, Ted Smollens was at the office, putting in an eight-hour day.

Eight hours was light activity as far as Ted was concerned, the equivalent of a walk around the block. Sixteen, seventeen hours – now *that* was work. That was real *Übermensch* hours. And to Ted, being an M & A guy meant being an *Übermensch* – a superman-style warrior on the corporate battlefield.

M & A – mergers and acquisition. The takeover division of every major financial house. The elite force. The SAS or the Green Berets of big business who went in to capture a company for a client, and seized it by whatever legal means necessary. You played hard. You played rough. And if 'achieving your objective' meant gutting your adversary, so be it. Because, as an M & A guy, you didn't mind a little bloodshed.

At the age of thirty-five, Ted Smollens was one of the top M & A guys on Wall Street. He raked in a cool $750,000 a year for his pains. And – as he told me over a scoop or three of Chivas in a bar on this day after Christmas – in the fourteen years since we'd both graduated from college, the secret of his success had been adopting a 'take no prisoners' philosophy in his professional life.

'You don't survive in my game,' Ted said, 'unless you believe in playing to win; in maintaining an edge over everyone else around you.'

Maintaining an edge. To Ted, there was something quasi-spiritual about this statement. It didn't simply explain his business strategy; it also defined his credo, his world-view. Maintaining an edge wasn't only about pulling in a mega-salary; it also meant living in the right house in the right suburb of Connecticut with his wife Beth and their two girls. And it meant being able to fund such leisure-time activities as collecting vintage motorcycles or propelling himself across Long Island Sound at 120 mph in one of his speedboats.

But while his part-time flirtation with internal combustion engines hinted at the macho-romantic side of his character, Ted was, at heart, simply a high-octane version of that classic American figure – the man who had embraced corporate culture with a vengeance, and had flourished within its confines. When he walked into the bar where we were meeting, I couldn't help but think: Ted really has become Mr Big. Maybe this was due to his new-found stockiness – the small deposit of fat beneath his square jaw; the vertical symmetry between the edge of his shoulders and the edge of his waistline. Or maybe it was the topcoat he was wearing – a rich navy blue double-breasted number in pure cashmere. It was a coat with a thousand-dollar price tag, a coat which acknowledged the influence and authority of its wearer.

In college, Ted had always attempted to project a solid 'good guy' persona, but he never quite pulled it off. I often wondered if this had something to do with the fact that he was the only member of our class to strut around campus in Gucci loafers. Perhaps it was bound up in his reputation as a tennis jock who was full of genial good will until it came to taking you on in singles. I once had the dubious pleasure of facing him across an asphalt court and being racket-whipped 6-0, 6-2. What was fascinating about this rout was the systematic way Ted carried out the task at hand. It didn't matter that we were simply playing a friendly couple of sets. Nor was I challenging him in order to test his manhood. He was, without question, the superior player – and he was simply going to demonstrate his superiority by blasting me off the court. Once the demolition job was done, he gave me a few collegial pointers about improving my game and then suggested we get ourselves a six-pack of Bud.

No wonder Ted was attracted to M & A – it perfectly suited his combative temperament, his belief that to play really *was* to win. As he sat down and ordered a large Scotch, I asked him if he was still playing gunslinger on the courts. He tugged at his lumpish waistline.

'Hard to move around the courts these days wearing an inner tube,' he said. 'Anyway, speedboat racing is as big a kick, and you don't get winded.'

He then launched into a long discourse about the $60,000 speedboat he had moored near his home, getting very Massachusetts Institute of Technology when it came to talking about its fuel-injected turbocharged engine, and its state-of-the-art getrag transaxle. I also heard all about the twelve vintage choppers that made up his motorcycle collection, and how he was thinking of popping over to London next month to negotiate the purchase of a 1952 Vincent Black Lightning. Then he told me about a very high-level takeover he was brokering at the moment (involving a small but highly lucrative pet food consortium with factories strung out across Alabama and Mississippi). After this, a few minutes were spent hearing about the likelihood of him breaking into the seven-figure income stratum next year, before I got a blow-by-blow account of how he met his wife (a former air hostess) when she served him a selection of Polynesian titbits while he was jetting first-class to Honolulu seven years ago.

Ted underscored this narrative of his achievements with the same laid-back tone that I remembered so well from our student days. He wanted me to be left in no doubt that he was a success – and he was going to keep on serving conversational ace after conversational ace until he was satisfied that I'd got the point. Yet, when I finally acknowledged his accomplishments – by saying something oily about how he seemed to be flourishing – his reply was a little bemusing.

'My life is crap.'

Then, after a substantial pause and an even more substantial belt of Scotch, he said, 'My two girls have just been diagnosed with leukaemia.'

The girls were twins, aged four. Around six months before, they both began to develop little lumps under their arms. Initially, Ted and Beth thought they'd come down with some sort of weird contagious infection (after all, why else would they be sharing almost identical symptoms?). But when they both began to shed weight and turn anaemic, alarm bells went off and their paediatrician dispatched them to hospital for tests.

The results were devastating: the girls were both suffering from an ultra-rare strand of leukaemia which, though containable for the moment, would be fatal within the next ten years. There was no tangible reason why the twins should have developed this disease: neither Beth's nor Ted's family had a history of lymphatic cancer. According to the eight or so specialists they'd seen to date, it was sheer chromosomal bad luck that it had manifested itself within them both almost simultaneously.

Ted said his wife had almost become unhinged when the news finally sank in. He, on the other hand, contained his shock by adopting a very methodical, very M & A approach to this calamity. This meant learning everything he could about leukaemia. As I listened to him discourse at length on the gross proliferation of leucocytes in the lymphatic system, I realized the extent of his frantic scholarship. He'd personally spoken to the dozen top leukaemia research specialists in the States; he'd read every study of the disease he could get his hands on; his girls had been seen by 'world class' medicos in New York, Zurich, Hamburg, Berkeley, and at the Mayo Clinic. In short, Ted was taking on his daughters' leukaemia the way he used to take on a tennis opponent: he was going to hit it with everything he had in his arsenal.

Although Ted did his best to sound controlled as he spoke about the catastrophe that had befallen his family, I sensed that behind his unexpressed (but clearly evident) anguish was a deep sense of confusion at the random nature of this disaster. Things were not supposed to turn out this way.

After all, Ted had worked so hard at getting all the components of his professional and emotional worlds just right. It's a deeply American trait, this widely-held notion that, to succeed in the world, you must have a game plan; a clearly defined agenda through which you will strive to achieve your very own set of goals. Listening to Ted speak about the way his carefully ordered universe had been undermined by a couple of faulty chromosomes put me in mind of something V.S. Pritchett once wrote about the American mind: that the major legacy of our Puritan heritage is 'the belief that you can build your life and work it out, conscientiously, bit by bit. The task is enormous; it is often dulling; but that is the price you pay for the perfectibility of man. There is no conception of tragedy; something just went wrong.'

Something had gone seriously wrong in Ted's life, and what gave his crisis even greater poignancy was his growing realization that he couldn't 'fix' the problem. No wonder he felt so helpless. Like all Americans of his class and educational background, he had been taught that the pursuit of excellence was a noble one, and that an essential part of this pursuit was learning how to be a handyman when it came to keeping the internal fabric of your life in order. But whereas Ted was fully capable of, say, repairing a contractual flaw when negotiating a takeover bid, or rectifying a problem on the marital front, if one arose, he could do nothing to remedy the genetic accident that had befallen his children.

This sense of powerlessness had not only kindled his grief and frustration, it also set Ted thinking long and hard about the subject of money. For money plays a central role in the American quest for perfectibility. It is the fuel which propels us forward in our search for a small patch of Utopia to call our own. And though the 1980s were rightly labelled a money-obsessed decade, we often forget that money and self-fulfilment have always been truly inseparable companions in American society – which means that, when circumstances beyond our control wreak havoc with our so-called life strategies, we often find ourselves suffering from a grave crisis of faith in an ethos which equates the getting of wealth with the getting of happiness.

Things were not supposed to turn out this way. The longer I listened to Ted, the more I sensed that this hard-nosed corporate raider believed his children's illness had rendered his life a failure. His pursuit of wealth had been bound up in the pursuit of an ideal family life – and that dream had now been devastated by the random malevolence of disease. It was, in many ways, like listening to a latter-day Puritan who had toiled to create his own little City on a Hill, only to have it ravaged by plague. Had this been the Massachusetts of 1638, Ted would have begged that angry, no-nonsense God hovering above colonial Boston for forgiveness, promising to atone for whatever sin had brought this curse upon his house. But as this was the Manhattan of the 1990s, all he could do was sip more Scotch and talk about the need to work harder, to make more money. Money would buy his kids more 'world class' medical treatment. Money, he desperately hoped, would eventually buy them a cure.

Like so many of his compatriots, Ted still wanted to believe that money could fix things. And he dreaded being proved wrong.

Ted had to dash off to make the 7.03 from Grand Central, but I hung on in the bar, nursing the remnants of my Scotch. Nearby, two men sat at a booth, tossing down thimbles of vodka.

'He trades like a fuckin' Arab,' one of them said.

'Whaddaya mean by that?'

'I mean what I say – he's an Arab when it comes to doin' a deal.'

'How does an Arab do a deal?'

'Barters your ass into a corner, that's how.'

'Arabs know about stuff like bartering?'

'Hey, asshole – Arabs *invented* bartering. You want to see where the art of the deal comes from, you go to an Arab country.'

I took note of the gentleman's advice . . . and acted upon it a few days later.

THREE

The Souk

He was standing outside my hotel on the Avenue Hassan II, a dude around thirty with a gold front tooth and mirrored sunglasses which caught the full rebounding glow of the North African sun. A denim jacket was draped over the shoulders of his jellaba. As he approached me, he thrust a fist in my face. This was his way of showing me his wares, for wrapped around his clenched fingers were a trio of imitation Parisian timepieces. A trio of Casablanca Cartiers.

'You buy,' Mr Cartier said. It was not a question; it was an order.

'No thanks,' I said, and tried to sidestep him.

'I offer you a bargain,' he said, blocking my path.

'What kind of bargain?'

'One thousand dirhams for a Cartier.'

'That's nearly a hundred pounds,' I said. 'Forget it.'

'You go to a shop here in Casa, you pay fifteen thousand dirhams for a new Cartier – that's fifteen hundred pounds your money. So I am offering you a fantastic price.'

'And you're also offering me an imitation.'

'Which is why I am offering you such a fantastic price.'

I had to smile at such candid chicanery. 'I'll give you a hundred dirhams for it.'

'That is a stupid price,' Mr Cartier said, smiling back. 'Eight hundred.'

'Talk to you later,' I said, and began to head off down the avenue. Mr Cartier followed in hot mercantile pursuit.

'Seven-fifty,' he said.

'No sale,' I said, picking up speed.

'You cannot go!' he shouted. 'We have a market!'

He was right, of course. By countering his offer with one of my own, I had essentially erected a set of price parameters, between which we would arrive at some sort of consensus when it came to negotiating the sale of the Casablanca Cartier. In short, I had created a market. But I didn't have time to barter in this marketplace, as I was off to catch the opening of another one – and one which, according to my very authentic Swatch, had begun ten minutes ago.

'Maybe we'll do business later,' I called back to Mr Cartier as I broke into a full-fledged sprint down the Avenue Mohammed V. Five breathless minutes later I made it to the steps of an imposing, if somewhat down-at-heel, Moorish building. Its intricate lattice windows and carved arches, and the string of fairy lights crisscrossing its façade, made it look like an architectural refugee from the casbah that had somehow ended up in the middle of Casablanca's modern, neo-colonial commercial district. Crashing through its carved doors, I discovered that I had the floor of the Casablanca bourse entirely to myself. Although it was Wednesday, the building was empty, silent, shrouded in an abandoned weekend atmosphere. As I leaned against a wall and listened to my out-of-shape heart play timpani in rhythm with my hyperventilating lungs, I silently cursed the hotel desk clerk who had assured me that the market would be alive and kicking at half past eight.

Still, there was something splendidly odd about having the floor of an entire stock exchange to oneself. Especially since the Casablanca bourse was such a curious set-up. I found myself in a large, high-vaulted room that was pure 1940s. Along the sides of this chamber were two rows of small mahogany office cubicles, with frosted glass windows and brass nameplates adorning each door. A blackboard the size of a Panavision film screen was suspended in the middle of the room. Directly below this chalkface was a steel walkway that evidently accommodated the unfortunate individual whose job it was to ride it during trading hours and chalk up prices.

The walls of the bourse were a grimy hospital white. The domed ceiling showed the after-effects of a burst pipe, and a patch or two of soundproof tiling had come unstuck and dangled ominously overhead. The floor was covered in scuffed, geriatric linoleum, and in one of the cubicles I spied an old-style manual adding machine and a thick, dust-encrusted ledger. The Casablanca bourse wasn't low-tech; it was no-tech.

'Bonjour.'

I was no longer alone. I had been joined by a rail-thin man in his late thirties with a long, melancholic face and black slicked-back hair – a North African Stan Laurel. He strode purposefully towards me and introduced himself as Mr Kettani, the assistant manager of the bourse. After we had shaken hands, he touched his heart with his right hand and bowed slightly – the formal mode of greeting in all Arab societies. Then he asked me my business.

'I was hoping to see the bourse in action,' I said. 'But I sense that I am a little early.'

Mr Kettani smiled. 'Two and a half hours early for *la séance*.'

'*La séance?*' I asked.

'The trading session,' Mr Kettani said. 'It begins at eleven.'

'And goes on until . . . ?'

'Eleven-thirty,' he said matter-of-factly.

'A thirty-minute trading day?'

Mr Kettani smiled again. 'This is not Wall Street, my friend. Anyway, half an hour is more than enough time for the brokers to take care of their business for the day.'

'What happens after eleven-thirty?' I asked.

'The bourse closes for the day and the brokers go to lunch. Usually until three.'

'A relaxed regime,' I said.

'Compared to London or New York or Paris, we are rather tranquil. But compared to the way business is done in Marrakesh or Fez, we are considered overworked.'

Mr Kettani said that the thirty-minute trading day had been

the norm ever since the *bourse de valeurs* first opened its doors in 1929. From its inception, it had been under the control of the Ministry of Finance, which only allowed twenty banks and private companies to trade in gold, foreign currencies, treasury bonds, and the few semi-state companies listed on the exchange. However, all this was about to change, thanks to that dreaded 1980s word – privatization.

'The Ministry has decided to Thatcherize us,' Mr Kettani said. 'Big Bang in Casa. The government is going to sell all its participation in semi-state companies, and completely deregularize the bourse, with more companies trading on the exchange, more stocks and bonds listed. And we've also been authorized to completely change the look of the bourse. So we're planning to heighten the Moroccan décor, but also to bring in computerized trading with up-to-the-minute equipment. Take a look around you. In twelve months, all this will seem like an antique. In twelve months, we will be high-tech.'

I scanned the tumbledown confines of the Casablanca bourse, trying to imagine it rigged out in Hotel Moroccan décor and flashing IBM screens. Then I caught sight of the man who had ultimately ordered the privatization of the bourse, H.R.H. King Hassan II, who was looking down upon the exchange floor from within a gilded frame. He was dressed in his 'man of commerce' clothes – a pinstriped Savile Row suit – and had a genial '*L'état c'est moi*' smile pasted on his face. Mr Kettani obviously saw me giving the photograph of the King the once-over, as he said:

'His Majesty takes a great interest in our activities here. And he believes a modern country needs a modern bourse, *n'est-ce pas?*'

'Absolutely,' I agreed.

'You will come back at eleven for *la séance?*' Mr Kettani asked. 'We haven't had a visitor from London in five years.'

Casablanca: the white house. White light. White brick. White breezeblock. A chalky concrete city which literally sweated from every pore. Every new building seemed to have a big damp patch across its façade, a blotchy stain of perspiration which hinted at gimcrack construction. Looking at those sweating office blocks was like looking at a hot-under-the-collar foreign businessman marooned in North Africa, his alienness emphasized by the telltale wet patches under the arms of his drip-dry summer suit.

Casablanca. *Une ville économique*. Financial capital of the Maghreb. A city of suits.

It was the suits that caught my eye as I left the bourse for my first proper perambulation through the city centre. Everywhere you turned there were men in two-piece pinstripes or Prince of Wales checks or dark shiny serge striding purposefully down the commercial boulevards. They all carried briefcases and had cigarettes super-glued to their lips. Even more intriguing was the significant number of besuited women on the streets – a hint that this was one Muslim society which hadn't yet painted itself into a fundamentalist cul-de-sac. And, even if many of these male and female suits seemed a decade or two behind present-day fashion, they all conspired to remind you that Casablanca was *une ville d'affaires*. Rabat may be the Moroccan city of diplomacy, Marrakesh and Fez the cities of mystique, but Casablanca was the town dedicated to the pursuit of the dirham through the gadgetry of late-twentieth-century finance. It was here that Morocco threw off its Byzantine vestments and reached for a Vodaphone.

I wandered down the Avenue Mohammed V. Like the rest of the business district, it was an architectural *mélange* of contemporary concrete and shabby holdovers from the days of French rule. There was a slightly fatigued feel to this central *quartier*, a sense that everything could use a lick of paint, and that a fresh paving stone or two wouldn't go amiss on the chewed-up pavements. But I was somewhat seduced by this slovenliness, this feeling that I had arrived in a high finance town which often forgot to tuck its shirt-tail into its trousers, which had a permanent five o'clock shadow.

I got lost in a maze of 1930s shopping arcades which eventually spat me out onto Boulevard Prince Moulay Abdallah – a pedestrian precinct crammed with shops trading in imitation leather goods (*ersatz* Cartier wallets and Louis Vuitton luggage), Van Giels suits and bejewelled daggers. This was Casablanca's Bond Street – its souk for the *beau monde*. But perhaps the most telling feature was the number of shops trading in computer equipment. Places with names like Multilog and Le Laptop, their windows crammed with floppy discs and Dot Matrix printers. Inside, salesmen demonstrated the multi-function capabilities of the Epson LX800 to bemused customers.

A street or two away was Chicago Electronics, which specialized in systolic blood-pressure meters. I poked my head inside and asked the salesman if he was actually shifting these microchippy blood-pressure cuffs.

'We sell a couple each week,' he said. 'Casablanca is full of businessmen. And when you have a city full of businessmen, you have a city full of stress. Which means you also have a city acutely conscious of high blood pressure.' He also informed me that if I was in the market for a top-of-the-range systolic meter with its own computerized printout, he could give me a 25 per cent discount as long as I paid in hard currency.

A city full of stress, acutely conscious of high blood pressure. This was Casablanca? The cosmopolitan casbah of yore? And yet, every newspaper kiosk I passed was crammed with back issues of a French health magazine called *Collection Allo Docteur* which covered topics like '*Comment Vaincre Tabac en 5 Jours*', or '*Maigrir en 28 Jours*'. Here, in the metropolis of mythic film lore, the Moroccan professional classes now fretted over their cigarette intake and the inner tube of flab encircling their midsection. No wonder so many outsiders despised Casablanca's present-day incarnation. The illicit, romantic port had been taken over by technocrats. The suits were now in charge, and they were hypertense.

But, as I came to discover, nothing was exactly as it seemed in Casablanca. The city showed you one aspect of itself and convinced you that you had gained its measure, then tossed up another image which utterly contradicted your previous conclusions. In this sense, it was a duplicitous town, a place which always kept you guessing.

Consider the scene at Fiori's, a café on the edge of the processional boulevard which housed the main offices of Casa's big banks and insurance companies. At first sight, Fiori's was Euro-trash Central: honchos in Agnes B suits; young Moroccan women in tight lycra dresses which seemed to have been heat-sealed to their torsos. 'This is North Africa?' I asked myself. 'This is an Islamic state?' I ducked into Fiori's while killing time prior to the opening of the bourse, and ended up sharing a table with a young merchant banker named Yusuf: fluent in three languages, educated in Switzerland and France, a smooth, eminently polished conduit between the Arab world and the West. He was also supremely chatty, telling me he'd been up half the night with his eighteen-month-old son and that he was treating himself to a late, leisurely breakfast before dealing with the bank – a bank which his family had been running for three generations. He also said that he was originally from the city of Fez, and gave me a quick introductory lesson in the Moroccan social structure:

'You know, there are three main classes in Morocco, and they are all based upon regions. There are the Fassis – which are my group – from Fez. They are the most francophile of all Moroccans, and largely emigrated to Casa for business purposes. They still try to bring up their children in the French way, sending them to French schools. Then there are the Berbers from the south of the country, who are very good small businessmen. Every corner shop you see in Morocco is Berber-run. They are very straight to deal with, but very, very slow. And finally there are the country people, who are simply backward. Like I said, the classes in Morocco are more regionalized than anything else.'

Yusuf came from a vast Fassi family. His grandfather alone

had had four wives and twenty-five children. Although Yusuf was sent to schools in Berne and Fontainebleau, his father had insisted that he spend every university holiday back in Morocco – shrewdly reckoning that if he allowed his son to stray too long in a big bad European world brimming with temptations, it would be hard to rein him back in to the family bank. But Yusuf said that even in the years when he was working for his Berne baccalaureate and his Fontainebleau MBA he always accepted that his destiny was to be a banker in Casa.

'It was my obligation as a son to join the family bank. How could I refuse my father's wishes?'

Yusuf was a man well acquainted with the idea of obligations. He'd been obliged to study business while overseas, and to look no further than the family bank when it came to employment, and to marry a Fassi girl of his own class, as it was simply inconceivable for him to consider a liaison with a woman from another corner of the country ('I have cousins who married Berber girls,' he said darkly, 'but none of them are happy'). He'd even been obliged to name his first-born son after his late father, who had died of cancer earlier that year.

Obligations, obligations. They were keeping Yusuf's stomach in a state of perpetual somersault.

'I've had a constant pain in my stomach for three years,' he suddenly said. 'It began one night in March of 1988, and it's refused to go away since then – to the point where I sometimes think I must have a faucet in my gut which drips a drop of acid every ten minutes or so. Of course, it makes sleep incredibly difficult, though I must say that, after three years, I am getting used to it.'

I asked Yusuf if he had sought medical assistance for this rather drastic condition.

'Of course I have been to doctors. In fact, I have been to every specialist in Morocco. I've had barium meals, ultrasound, even exploratory surgery, and they've found nothing. Tension, they tell me – but they can find no physiological evidence of a stomach disorder. I've tried dozens of medicines, milk diets, herbal infusions, relaxation exercises – none of them have helped. So I am trying something new at the moment . . . prayer. *Insh'allah*, my stomach will be silent soon.'

Yusuf mentioned that his stomach had turned malevolent on him around the time that his father was diagnosed as having terminal lung cancer. But I wondered if his chronic dyspepsia was also linked to his rigid belief in obligations, in acting out the role that was expected of him. As someone who had tasted life outside Morocco's stringent social order, he'd had first-hand experience of a world due north of here – a place where it wasn't considered a form of betrayal if you refused to join the family business, and where you didn't have to marry a woman from within your family's circle of friends. Did he ponder that less restrictive world while he counted the cracks in the paintwork above his bed at four in the morning and waited for the next Exocet of bile to hit the abdominal wall? Or did he simply accept his pre-ordained life? Listening to Yusuf talk, I was struck by the way in which he was precariously balanced between two disparate realms. Like the city in which he lived, he was decked out in the costume of a late-twentieth-century businessman, and spoke an international business language, peppering his conversation with references to Third World debt restructuring, the collapse of the junk bond market, and the versatile virtues of Apple Macintosh software. He even had the disarming, quasi-American habit of assuming immediate intimacy with a stranger by telling him his life story. And yet, lurking behind this cosmopolitan veneer was an inflexible traditionalism, a conviction that the rules of life he'd been brought up to obey were the only rules to play by – especially since he came from the charmed upper echelon of his society.

'You're married,' he said, noticing my wedding ring.

'Six years,' I said.

'How many children?'

'None.'

'I'm sorry,' he said, suddenly embarrassed.

'Why should you be sorry?' I asked.

'Because it must be very upsetting for you, having these . . .' (he paused briefly, choosing his words with great care) . . . 'medical difficulties.'

'What medical difficulties? My wife and I don't have children because we don't want children. Not yet, anyway.'

'But what does she do all day?'

'She has her own business, her own company.'

'You allow this?'

'It's not a matter of me "allowing" her to do anything. She does what she wants to do.'

'And you don't mind?'

'Why should I mind? It's her life.'

'Unbelievable,' Yusuf said.

As we spoke, two young women got up from the table next to ours and left. A pair of businessmen headed towards the now-free table, but Yusuf said something to them in Arabic which had the immediate effect of making them seek out another place to sit.

'What was that all about?' I asked.

'I told them that women were sitting in those chairs before them, so they naturally had to find somewhere else to sit.'

I ventured a 'Why?'

'It would be very bad for a man to sit where a woman had sat. It would be a sign of disrespect for his wife. It would be courting temptation.'

Now it was my turn to choose my words carefully. 'You actually believe all that?' I asked.

'Of course I believe it,' Yusuf said. 'It's true.'

Nothing was as it seemed in Casablanca.

I returned to the bourse a few minutes before eleven. The floor of the exchange was still empty, but then the brokers began to drift in. The first through the doors was a French gentleman in an elderly double-breasted suit with a small red *légion d'honneur* discreetly pinned to a buttonhole. He was a hefty patriarch, of the sort you expect to see out inspecting his vineyards in Provence.

'*Le père de la bourse,*' Mr Kettani whispered to me before going over to greet him.

The father of the exchange (who, I later learned, had been born in Casablanca of Marseillais parents and had been trading here since 1947) came over to shake my hand. The next two traders through the door also greeted me with handshakes after giving their salutations to *le père de la bourse*. They were both in their thirties – sallow-faced accountant types who could easily have passed muster in Amersham. Following them was a snazzy *homme du monde* in cashmere, a thin leather documents case tucked under his arm. Then two women brokers made an appearance. One was semi-spinsterish, the other totally spinsterish. The total spinster was around forty, wearing thick stockings and dark elderly clothes. The semi-spinster was dressed identically, only she was ten years younger and snapped gum incessantly. As they entered, they too worked the floor, shaking hands with everyone present.

The business of salutation was an important pre-trade ritual on the Casablanca bourse. Watching this elaborate form of greeting (involving both parties clasping hands, then touching their respective hearts, then bowing slightly) was like witnessing a form of courtly mercantilism at work. To enter the exchange and not greet everybody else individually would be considered a horrendous breach of etiquette. For here, a trading floor was not an arena of competitiveness; it was a club. Dealers didn't eye each other up as potential rivals, nor did anyone look as if they were cruising towards coronary occlusion. The atmosphere of personal and collective desperation – so common within the confines of most major exchanges – was absent on the Casablanca bourse. Instead, there was an air of collegial insouciance, an unspoken understanding that the buying and selling of a few shares wasn't a life-and-death matter. It was simply something you did for half an hour each day.

Before the routine began, the twenty or so dealers spent a good fifteen minutes chatting with each other. Gossipy discussions in French (the language of the exchange) broke out around the floor – about the price of gold that morning in Paris, about the disastrous opening on the Tokyo exchange (the worst since the Crash of 1987), and about how the franc was faring this week. I couldn't help noticing that Casablanca's traders were very *au fait* with the barometric pressure readings from the world's major financial marketplaces. Just as they were *au fait* with each other's golf handicap. In fact, their interest in their recent form on the course at Mohammedia (the best in the Casablanca region) exceeded their concern about the price Cosumar (the semi-state sugar company) was selling at this morning. For the two dozen or so stocks and bank bonds traded on the Casablanca bourse were carefully regulated – to the point where, according to Mr Kettani, prices could only fluctuate by 3 per cent on any given trading day (though, as he pointed out, 'A 3 per cent drop for thirty straight days might cause some upset'). In short, the Casablanca bourse was a realm of non-existent financial risk. The traders were offering their clients safe investments which yielded minimal, but steady dividends. No one could use the bourse to flex any fiscal muscles or indirectly to let the world know that they had a large sexual organ. It was, instead, a place of modest aspirations where everyone silently agreed to maintain a collective equilibrium.

The first signal that trading was about to begin came when Mr Kettani moved through the clusters of dealers handing out mimeographed sheets listing the day's opening prices. Then, around a quarter of an hour later than advertised, a bell sounded – the sort of bell that wouldn't have been out of place in a boxing ring. *Que la séance commence.*

Even though trading had officially opened, everybody continued talking for five more minutes. Then another officer from the bourse climbed onto the library trolley beneath the big blackboard and began methodically calling out the names of all the stocks and bonds listed there. The traders drifted towards the wooden ring in the centre of the floor, still chatting away amongst themselves. This steady stream of gossip continued throughout the entire *séance*, and was only occasionally interrupted by someone shouting out '*Je vends!*' or '*J'achète!*' when a stock they were interested in was named. Often, entire stocks went untraded as the caller worked his way through the list of shares on offer. Once or twice, a small, momentary struggle ensued between two traders who got into an exceedingly polite *Je vends/J'achète* shouting match.

Such moments of barter-drama were rare indeed, and caused only a mild flurry of interest amongst the brokers. As the caller continued bellowing the name of every listed stock, the atmosphere of the bourse began to resemble a spacious, uncrowded bar where the collective hum of animated conversation was infrequently pierced by someone shouting for a drink.

After thirty minutes the last stock was announced, the bell was rung again, and Mr Kettani and his assistants handed out chits which the dealers quickly filled out, registering their buys and sells of the day. Then it was time for a final round of ritualistic politesse, as everybody shook hands yet again and bowed farewell. Suddenly, the floor was deserted, as the traders left this high-vaulted cavern of shadows and walked out into the hard North African light.

La séance est terminée. And the Casablanca bourse was still for another day.

I left the bourse and pointed myself in the direction of the souk. To get there, I had to walk back to the end of the Avenue Mohammed V and then go subterranean, taking a staircase down into a modern subway which passed under a restless road. There was something splendidly absurd about the idea of descending from a concrete shopping precinct into a concrete pedestrian passageway, crossing under a maelstrom of traffic, and then re-emerging above the surface into a fully-functioning North African bazaar – particularly as this souk

was a predictably chaotic swirl. There was the usual webwork
of narrow dirt-paved laneways, the usual jumble of tradesmen
lining them, and fruit merchants negotiating their donkey
carts through the maze. Women in black were performing
remarkable balancing acts with groceries piled high atop their
heads. Shops spilled out into the gutter. And a potpourri of raw
sewage and rotting vegetables made the air a thick, glutinous
substance which adhered to my clothes, my face, my hair.

What made the scene bemusing was the fact that it was
overshadowed by the twenty-five-storey glass-and-concrete
Casablanca Grand Hyatt Hotel. If you kept your eyes at
street level, you were presented with a panorama of goats
running wild, of vendors who hawked doorknobs for a living,
of jerry-built shacks, of barefoot children wading in pools of
stagnant water. Once you looked to the sky, however, the
immediate vista was defined by an over-sized satellite dish
with the letters CNN emblazoned in its centre. Across the
Arab world you'll constantly find such juxtapositions of the
modern and the primitive, the hi-tech and the antediluvian. But
here in Casablanca there was the added incongruity of having a
contemporary commercial zone and an elemental souk linked
by a subway. What's more, just as the city's modern shopping
district traded in imitation Cartier and Louis Vuitton accessor-
ies, so the souk had an entire quarter devoted to bogus Reebok
trainers, Wrangler jeans and Sony Walkmans. Casablanca: an
imitative city, reproducing fraudulent versions of brand-name
consumer booty and then flogging it at knock-down prices. A
town of counterfeit Western mercantilism sold to the highest
bidder.

Venturing deeper into the souk, I came upon a small
rectangular patch of open ground made malodorous by the
neighbouring presence of an open sewer. Competing with
the cheering odour of human faeces were the slightly more
palatable aromas of saffron, ginger, nutmeg, turmeric and
cinnamon. The spice market was open for business. It was
an assortment of crude, roughly hewn tables piled high with

contrasting sandcastles of russet red, canary yellow, terracotta brown. The merchants in charge of these kaleidoscopic knolls were men in their seventies, their faces as lined as cracked bas-reliefs and their gums devoid of teeth. Each of them was armed with an old-style counterweight measuring scale and a larynx of exceptional power, enabling them to cry out commodity prices over the entire din of the bazaar. When a buyer approached, the merchant would bow, touch his heart, and then begin the bartering game.

'Five grams of cinnamon – ten dirhams.'

'Try six.'

'The best I can do is seven and a half.'

'Okay, I buy.'

I buy – *j'achète*. I turned to another merchant scooping up a handful of ginger and depositing it in the brass bucket on his weighing scales.

'Fourteen dirhams,' he told his black-veiled customer. She shook her head vigorously.

'Twelve, then,' the merchant said.

Another shake of her shrouded head.

'Eleven, last offer. *Vous achetez?*'.

A nod of agreement was now forthcoming.

Here, in this realm of the spices, a 'market price' was being created – a set of fiscal frontiers within which to reach a consensus. It was the language of the stock exchange translated to the basic act of buying seasoning for food. And it was the bourse which had obviously imitated the ways of the souk: inheriting from it the formal mode of greeting between buyer and seller; the open outcry style of trading; the rapid manner in which the value of a commodity was established and agreed upon in order to leave both parties with a sense that the deal was a fair one. After all, what is a bourse but a souk where the actual goods on offer are absent, and where middlemen do the dickering for the buyer and the seller?

And in Casablanca, the souk was everywhere.

★   ★   ★

The next day I returned to the bourse for another thirty-minute *séance* of high financial drama. It was an action-packed half-hour. By the time the final bell rang, exactly eight transactions had taken place – and the price of five of the stocks traded remained absolutely unchanged. Once again, much time was taken up with hand-on-the-heart greetings. Once again, the dealers stood in an informal circle and engaged in a collective schmooze while the caller worked his way through the listed stocks. I was standing next to a dealer named Mahmoud Al Atrash: a bespectacled, librarian-ish forty-year-old with a hangdog moustache and an ageing houndstooth jacket who worked for a mid-sized bank. He was probably the liveliest trader on the floor that morning, buying three lots of shares and engaging in a minor bidding war with one of the two spinsterish woman dealers. As they tussled briefly over the share price of Brasserie Maroc, the country's leading brewery, the man on the library trolley was kept unexpectedly busy with his chalk and eraser. Eventually, after two minutes of ping-pong banter (in which the price fluctuated between 220 and 225), the woman gave Mahmoud a look which all but said, 'Let's knock this off – it's getting near lunchtime.' Mahmoud, with a generous shrug of the shoulders, relented and halted his staccato cries of '*J'achète!*'

Afterwards, as I walked with Mahmoud down the Avenue Mohammed V, I asked him why he gave in to the other dealer so readily.

'It is simple, really,' he said. 'I had come into the bourse this morning with the intention of pushing the price of Brasserie Maroc up by three to five points for one of my customers. But when it reached 222, I was happy to stop, as I had basically accomplished what I wanted to accomplish.'

Somehow, I couldn't see a confirmed Wall Streeter adopting such a benign attitude towards 'the competition'. Then again, if you were a broker working a thirty-minute trading session in a carefully regulated market, you'd probably show benevolence towards your supposed rivals on the floor. Especially if you came from a culture which deemed it important to live according to the spirit of *maleesh*.

Maleesh is an Arabic word which means 'never mind'. It also sums up an entire world view: a belief that life's tensions and setbacks should be kept in their proper perspective, and should not cause you undue disquiet. Having done time in a few corners of the Arab world, I have always felt that one of the principal reasons for the mutual incomprehension between Western and Islamic societies was the inexplicability of *maleesh* to anyone outside Muslim life. In the West we constantly measure our lives in terms of achievement or failure. We demand results from life. In Islam, however, temporal existence is merely a passing hassle en route to eternal paradise – so why get worked up over the inconsequential here-and-now?

Therefore, when attempting to push up the price of Brasserie Maroc from 220 to 225, why provoke the perforation of your duodenum if you only manage to jack it up to 222? After all, it's only a commercial transaction, and you've got the basic result you wanted, so . . . *maleesh*. And even if you haven't achieved what you wanted to achieve, even if you've failed . . . *maleesh*. Never mind. A bad morning on the Casablanca bourse is but a grain of sand in the eye of Allah.

Initially, Mahmoud Al Atrash struck me as someone who very much abided by the *maleesh* philosophy when it came to the world of the bourse. But, like a true Casablancan, his seemingly straightforward image belied a more complex underside. Taking up his offer to see where he worked, I hopped a taxi with him to the sweaty white concrete block which housed his bank. After passing through a nondescript foyer we entered an office that was pure Eastern Europe – breezeblock walls painted a mental-institution green; meagre, low-wattage fluorescent lighting; a ramshackle collection of steel desks. Like the Casablanca bourse, this office was a near-throwback to the days when the abacus was the height of technology.

It was lunchtime, so all of Mahmoud's colleagues had headed

home. However, the bank's elderly tea man was still on duty, and Mahmoud persuaded him to bring us a pot of mint tea and some cakes before he too left for an afternoon siesta. We retreated into Mahmoud's office – which was nothing more than a cop-shop desk surrounded by a couple of cheap cardboard screens.

'Welcome to the trading division of the bank,' Mahmoud said.

'You're it?'

'I am it – a one-man show.'

Mahmoud had been the bank's one-man trading operation for the past five years. Before that, he'd been in its investment division. Before that, he'd done time in its corporate section. And before that . . . ?

'I was at university, reading political science. It is the done thing in Morocco – to go from university to a job with a company and to stay there for the rest of your working life. And my family are all professional people, so it was expected that I go to university, and that I become either a lawyer, a diplomat or a financier. It is very difficult to break out of family expectations in Morocco . . . just as it is also difficult to escape from a job once you are in it.'

Mahmoud went into banking because he thought it was a safe option, the ticket to a comfortable, bourgeois future. When he started realizing just *how* safe it was, he wangled his way into investments, and began quietly lobbying for the job as the bank's man on the bourse (the occupant of that role was about to retire after twenty-five years of daily thirty-minute trading sessions). Mahmoud knew the bourse wasn't exactly the most dynamic of financial arenas, but he'd heard rumours that the King – via the Ministry of Finance – was seriously weighing up the idea of privatizing the stock exchange. And the way Mahmoud figured it, this might eventually put him in a potentially lucrative position.

'It has taken five years of waiting, but we are now on the verge of a major change in the affairs of the bourse. Up until now, almost all the traders on the exchange have been attached to banks. Our clients are largely insurance companies, who have huge holdings in all the banks here, or private individuals who are either living in the country or are resident abroad with money still here in dirhams. Well, after privatization next year, the bourse will get bigger – around ten times bigger than it is now. There will be share issues, computerized trading, and at least ten new private trading companies. For Moroccan finance, this will be fantastic – the share issues will mean that a lot of ordinary middle-class Moroccans will get involved in the life of the bourse. So, after privatization, our public profile will be much higher.'

'And this will mean more money for you?' I asked.

'Perhaps,' Mahmoud said, with undisguised caginess. Then, after sticking his head around the cardboard divider to make certain that we were alone, he lowered his voice to confessional-box level.

'The actual answer to your question is this: if I stay on in the bank, I will continue to be paid the bad money I am paid now. Wages are not good here, even for senior personnel. And even though it was me who attracted almost all my customers to the bank, I get no bonus for bringing in new business. This is not very satisfactory from my standpoint, especially as I have a wife and two young children to support. And especially as last month I did a transaction which netted the bank the equivalent of my salary for the next fifteen years.

'If I go out on my own as a private trader, I can bring all my customers with me. And if the market develops the way we all believe it will develop, I should be making three times my present salary once I go it alone. Three times minimum.'

'So when are you going to quit the bank?' I asked.

Mahmoud immediately put a finger to his lips. 'I am only talking in purely speculative terms,' he said loudly, as if addressing some hidden microphone. 'Especially since I am so happy here.' But then, dropping his voice down a secretive octave or two, he said: 'I tell you this – the first thing I'm going to do when I finally do go independent is get myself a better office.'

Idriss Amin had a terrific office. Low-slung Swedish furniture. Tizio lamps. Bang and Olufsen telephones. An IBM PC with laser printer. A squat Mont Blanc pen strategically located at the midpoint of his tubular-steel and glass desk. A state-of-the-art corporate environment housed within a state-of-the-art corporate headquarters – all bleached wooden floors, crisp white walls, designer air vents in primary colours, and contemporary Moroccan abstract canvases. In the midst of this coolly calculated décor was Idriss Amin – resplendent in Daniel Hechter pinstripes – pumping my hand and saying, 'I'm the deals guy around here.'

The deals guy. I asked Idriss where he picked up his flawless English.

'Harvard,' he said. 'The B-School.'

He was around thirty, the son of a Moroccan diplomat. His childhood had been a succession of embassy compounds in Cairo, Riyadh, Washington and London, so it made sense that he was now ensconced in a financial compound, in charge of his own division. The deals division.

'After I finished Harvard, I had a lot of offers in the States, but when they offered me the deals job here, I really couldn't resist. Because, let's face it, there aren't too many deals guys like me in Morocco.'

Idriss was an investment banker in a major Casablanca merchant bank, an institution which, he staunchly maintained, had moved with the times.

'What this bank understands is the simple fact that Morocco's entire future is bound up in the private sector. We're like every other Third World country, in that we created a huge public sector after our independence. But the government – the King himself – now recognizes that the economy simply can no longer support redundant factories or maintain an absurd state bureaucracy. So what they're moving towards is a form of popular capitalism, where individual business initiative will be rewarded, and where every man can own shares. This is why the privatization of the bourse is so important, because it is seen as a symbol of the new economic times here. And, thank God, we are a relatively stable society – which, let's face it, is not exactly typical in this part of the world.

'But the King has always been very shrewd about things like keeping us largely an agricultural country – which means that, unlike Algeria or Tunisia, we don't have millions of backward rural people flooding into the cities looking for work. And we're very lucky that, in choosing to side with Western economic policies, the King also decided to stay Islamic at the same time – so, unlike Algeria at the moment, we're not threatened by Muslim fundamentalists, since we've maintained the tenets of the faith.'

'Are you yourself a devout Muslim?' I asked.

Idriss Amin thought that one over for a long moment. 'I am a modern Muslim,' he finally said. 'Islam is my faith, Allah is my God . . . and I also keep my eye firmly on the bottom line.'

The deals guy. With the Harvard vocab and the Continental tailoring. Back home in a town which was and wasn't an Islamic city, whose denizens behaved as if they were displaced Southern Europeans who had somehow ended up on the wrong side of the Mediterranean. Back home with a line of venture capital from a leading European investment bank. Back home with plans. Big plans.

'People aren't used to deal-makers in the Third World. But what this country needs is guys like me. Because deals guys make things happen. Like, if you come back to Casa this time next year, six new companies will be up and running, thanks to the venture capital deals I'm putting into place at the moment. And if the government is smart about it – if they start encouraging more deals guys like me to start looking for new lines of investment capital in Europe and the States – this place could open wide up. We've got the geographic position, the physical resources and the cheap labour to be a Singapore or a Taiwan for the Atlantic rim. For a start, we could turn a town like Tangier back into being an offshore city – a tax-free zone – and take it from there. Okay, okay, I know I'm probably talking craziness, especially since the economy has been closed here for years. But given time and the right sort of financial incentives, this whole country could be transformed.'

I thought about the canny corner-boys who peopled every Moroccan street, hassling foreigners into parting with a few dirhams for their services as guides. I thought about the men in the souk who eked out a living filling cigarette lighters or selling off bits of drainpipe. I thought about a previous journey I had made into the Moroccan interior, passing through villages where families of six lived in single-room huts and where the cadences of life hadn't really been touched by this most overwhelming of centuries. I thought about *maleesh* and its temperamental implications. Then I looked up at Idriss Amin and found myself in a different country. I asked: 'Are you really that optimistic about Morocco's ability to reinvent itself?'

'I know what you're thinking,' Idriss said. 'You're thinking I'm some Harvard boy who's been away from home too long . . . who's out of touch with the reality of his country. Well, I'll let you in on a little secret. See that guy out there?' He pointed out of his window to a man on the pavement hawking some merchandise on a makeshift table. 'You know what links him and me? The street. It's not laws that make a market. It's the street. And the reason I'm optimistic about this country at the moment is because business is booming on the street. The street is where the money is in Morocco. The street is the marketplace – our greatest commercial strength. If we could harness the dynamism of the street, we could – economically speaking – kick ass.'

I stared out at the kerbside merchant. He glanced in my direction, and we caught each other's eye. It was Mr Cartier – the man who stuck his fist in my face on my first day in Casa and demanded that I buy one of his imitation timepieces. He recognized me immediately, and waved his fist in the air – a fist around which was still wrapped a trio of Casablanca Cartiers. Idriss opened the window, and the merchant yelled at me:

'New offer . . . three hundred dirhams.'

'Offer two-fifty,' Idriss immediately advised.

'But I don't want the watch.'

'Did you make him an initial offer?'

'Yeah – one hundred.'

'And what was his first price?'

'A thou.'

'And you're complaining about having to pay two-fifty?'

'But, like I said, I don't want the watch . . . '

'Okay, so give the watch away. But make him the offer of two-fifty and enjoy . . . '

'Enjoy what?'

Idriss Amin looked at me as if I was the dumbest person alive. 'Enjoy the deal, of course.'

I shouted 'Two-fifty' out of the window. Mr Cartier hemmed and hawed. But then, with a shrug of his shoulders, he acknowledged that we had finally reached a consensus.

I said goodbye to the only Harvard-educated deals guy in Casablanca and hit the street. Where, of course, I bought the watch.

FOUR

Midnight Money

It is midnight in Sydney. A soft, moist summer night. The sort of antipodean night when your shirt plasters itself to your back, your brow is beaded with sweat, and the air is an aromatic scramble of bougainvillaea, sea salt, smouldering cigarettes, and the increasingly fetid remnants of a Thai take-away. You're sitting on the hardwood deck of a house in a suburb called Mosman. It's a hardwood deck which fronts a harbour inlet. Beneath it slosh the waters of the Pacific. Counterpointing this aquatic metronome is the airy percussion of wind chimes dangling from the half-dozen other hardwood decks curving around this cove. A cork is pulled from a bottle of Hunter Valley chardonnay, the fourth such cork to be pulled this evening. You and your hosts – a pair of married financiers in their early forties – toast each other. An agreeably boozy air hangs over the proceedings. And, casting yourself in the role of the envious spectator, you ask yourself why you live on such a tight, mildewy little island when all this could be yours – Lotus Land incarnate. *La dolce vita* at 34° South latitude.

But then somebody mentions the state of the country's economy and the Utopian bubble bursts. Paradise found . . . Paradise lost.

It is midnight in Sydney, and you are in a room with a view. A room floating twenty-seven levels above the city centre. A room the size of a football pitch with wrap-around windows. Stand in the centre of this room and gaze at the darkness beyond, and you can almost convince yourself that you are a passenger in a space station, fully equipped with a ton or two of high-tech equipment. Move closer to the thermapane and you are afforded a wide-screen panorama of a metropolitan terrain decked out in its evening apparel. The other office blocks of the CBD (the central business district) envelop you in a vertical fluorescent glow. Just beyond this perpendicular display, the curving black waters of the harbour are an illuminated Rorschach Test of mutable patterns. The scene reminds you that New World cities are at their most seductive after dark, when their high-rise, hard-edged modernity is softened by all those configurations of light stacked up in the sky. No wonder so many predatory appetites have been sharpened by the sight of this nocturnal cityscape. Sydney at night isn't simply alluring; it glows with venal promise.

Inside this room, however, no one is paying any attention to the view. Instead, the seven souls at work at this late hour focus their attention on the green figures that dance across their computer screens. They are all but umbilically attached to telephones, and are currently in consultation with New York, London, Paris, Frankfurt. The atmosphere is informal (denims, shorts and T-shirts are the sartorial norms), yet there is a quiet, unmistakable air of unease, reminiscent of films you've seen of military officers working late into the night in a command centre, tracking the movements of the enemy on an elaborate array of ultra-sophisticated equipment. There's the same sense of concentrated, witching-hour intensity to this tableau. Only here the 'enemy' under scrutiny is the marketplace. For this squad of after-hours foreign exchange dealers knows that their professional survival depends on how they manipulate those numbers.

'We're the dawn patrol,' says Robbo, the leader of the pack. 'We're the people who play with midnight money.'

Midnight money. When the dead of night ushers in a new day in Sydney, they've just finished lunch in London and breakfast in New York. While the markets of Australasia sleep, the Western bourses are awake and trading. So the dawn patrol of slumbertime dealers – clustered together in trading rooms like this one around Sydney – stalk the activities of the money markets in Europe and North America until night wakes up and the Far Eastern business day begins.

'We're up all night to set the positions that will start the morning's trading,' Robbo says. 'And when we're done . . . we go to the beach.'

It is midday in Sydney. The all-night dealers are now on the sands of Bondi, taking with them their beach-bum clothes, their hushed voices, their low-key intensity. Their places have been taken by the power-suited, armed with heavy-metal vocal chords. There are now around sixty dealers spread out across this electronic souk, and they are all talking at once. Sixty different conversations, all conducted with panicky brio. The roar of the gamble in motion.

It is the clamour that hits you first when you enter this dealing room. What captures your attention next is the realization that just about everyone on the premises is around twenty-five years old. All right, there is the occasional representative of the over-thirties, not to mention a couple of twenty-one-year-old financial ingenues. In general, though, the players here are in their prime mid-twenties. And, despite their vocal freneticism, they all have the look of a division one squad – that play-to-win confidence which comes with believing that they're the hottest, best-paid team on the block.

'They're the sexiest of the sexy,' Johnno says, surveying the trading floor in full swing. 'What's more, the bastards know it. And they come to work for us because of our reputation for being the Australian bank with *the* hot-shit trading room. We may not be the biggest bank in the country, but when it comes to dealing, we are *the* bank.'

Johnno's eyes again scan the floor. 'Of course, in the back of their minds, all these kids know that they're like athletes in their prime. And they also know that we'll keep them on the team as long as they maintain peak performance. But like most athletes, the majority of them will pass that peak by their mid-thirties, which means they'll be out of a job here.'

I asked Johnno – a man on the craggy precipice of middle age – how he'd managed to avoid getting dropped from the squad.

'Simple, really. I hung up my jersey and became a coach.'

Johnno liked sporting analogies. He also evidently favoured the conscious one-of-the-boys informality which a nickname like Johnno gave him. After all, his full name – Jonathan Winston Pendleton – exuded a certain Pommy formality, whereas 'Johnno' was pure unadulterated Ocker. And the guise of informality, I came to discover, was a key component of the Australian financial persona. By acting the good bloke, one could easily mask the go-for-the-jugular inclinations which had made Sydney the dynamic and irrepressibly malevolent financial arena it was today. Good blokes, I decided early on, were to be approached with care.

Johnno was undoubtedly a good bloke, but one who didn't try to overwhelm you with his amiability – a fact that led me to believe he was a relatively straight operator. The man was certainly no swank (his off-the-peg suit and salt-and-pepper beard gave him a rather junior-common-room demeanour), nor was he in love with his own perfume – as I discovered when I asked him whether there were any loose cannons amongst his dealers on the floor.

'We don't tolerate loose cannons around here. And if any dickhead tries to act the cowboy, we'll eat him for breakfast. In other words, there's no star system in this dealing room. I'm probably the highest-profile person on the floor, and I am definitely not high profile. I mean, I fell into this game by accident, and I try not to take it too bloody seriously.'

He was a Sydney boy, raised in that big geographic nowhere called 'the Westies', the Western Suburbs – mile after mile of tin-roofed bungalows far from the city's svelte coastline. To venture into the Westies was to grasp the realities of so many emigrant dreams: life in a cramped, jerry-built dwelling on the extreme outskirts of Australia's most radiantly slick city. Despite his patrician name, Johnno was the son of a clerk in the civil service. And he had only gone into banking after university because he had won a scholarship for tertiary education sponsored by one of the big Australian banks.

'Y'wanna know the only reason I went into the banking game? Five dollars. When I was leaving school, I was also offered a scholarship to uni by an insurance company, but the bank offered me one that paid five dollars more a week. The way I looked at it, that five bucks was a few extra beers a week. And after I got my degree, I ended up getting into trading thanks to complete dumb luck. My first job in the bank was as personal assistant to the General Manager – which meant that I was engaged in really high-powered activities like organizing a chauffeur for the bastard, or lying to his wife about his whereabouts. And around that time, the trading department (which was really nothing back then, 'cause we're talking almost fifteen years ago, the bloody dark ages of the Australian financial markets) went through one of its periodic purges, and a bunch of newcomers from within the bank decided to move in on it. The guy who got there first became the chief dealer. And since I arrived thirty minutes after him, I became the deputy chief dealer.'

From the start, the real amphetamine kick attached to trading foreign exchange was picking up the phone, saying yes to a multimillion dollar transaction, and knowing that the bank would have to back it up. 'Some of the people I started with simply couldn't handle the idea of dealing with seven zeros' worth of other people's money. They wanted to go back to the world of worrying about getting fifteen dollars in expenses from petty cash. But I was hooked from the start. Especially since dealing is all about two things – calculated decisiveness, and the ability never to look back. You've got to be able to weigh up the odds, take a decision, live or die by that decision, and move on.

'What we're talking about is instant rush. What have you

done today? How have you measured yourself against the market? Is your dong bigger than mine? That kind of enlightened competitiveness. The problem is, you can easily become an instant rush junkie, to the point where you completely run amok. That's why you have to know the parameters. You have to know when to rein yourself right in.'

Johnno was obviously an experienced corporate navigator when it came to knowing how far he could travel down a particular professional road before hitting a dead end. In his early thirties, he realized he was beginning to lose the edgy vigour which had made him a top trader for the previous decade. To avoid being put out to pasture like most dealers, he decided to move into management, and ended up assuming the role of coach to the players on the floor.

'I'm just like a football manager when it comes to picking and choosing my side. And though I usually choose graduates, I'll hire anybody who I think has it when it comes to trading Forex. I mean, the way I figure it, as long as you have tenacity and a quick mind, I can probably whip you into shape and make you the sort of dealer we like around here – by which I mean that you won't act like a stupid shit and you'll learn the basic rule of trading: quit when you're behind or when you're ahead. We don't want bad gamblers around here – bad gamblers always hang on in a game long after it's smart to leave it.'

The team mentality was an important facet of the trading room. According to Johnno, the players generally tended to socialize together after work and at the weekends. And if a trader was on the prowl for a little sexual comfort, he or she usually chose another trader to assume the role of temporary squeeze, as this also allowed them to engage in post-coital discussions about long-term prospects for the yen.

Johnno himself, however, now tried to distance himself from such a relentless involvement with the marketplace. He was married to a doctor and had a circle of friends who didn't care a pfennig about the state of the pfennig.

But, despite his conscious efforts to erect a *cordon sanitaire* between his private life and the trading floor, he hadn't been able to shake off certain habits – like the fact that he always answered the telephone with something approaching a scream, and that (according to his wife) it was impossible to have a conversation with him in a restaurant, as he possessed radar ears and was constantly listening in to what was going on at every other table around him.

'Y'see, the major difference between being a coach and being a player is that the player must always perform. And these kids realize that this is their five minutes in the sun; that, like the instant rush of making a deal, their whole career here is just one fast rush which will be over before they know it.'

'What do they do when they finally get the heave-ho?' I asked.

'It's strange, really, but the vast majority of them get out of the business altogether. I mean, you go over to North Sydney or up the coast and you'll find dozens of former traders doing things like running hot bread shops or bottle shops or wholesale nursery businesses.'

'Sounds like a bit of a comedown after the trading floor.'

'After you've played on a division one team,' Johnno said, 'everything is a comedown.'

Twenty-seven levels below Johnno's trading floor was the actual floor of the Sydney Stock Exchange. The trading area was off limits to everyone except brokers, but casual spectators and interested punters were allowed to observe the proceedings from behind a wide-screen sheet of soundproof glass. Watching the boys and girls go through their paces on this relatively small floor (about the same size as the bourse in Casablanca, with a similar old-style scoreboard dominating the scene) was like watching a soundless sport being played out by people at the peak of their performance. Johnno was right – this really was a game for young athletes. And they played it until that moment when they found they were losing their stamina, their competitive edge; when they woke up one morning and asked themselves, 'Why am I running so hard?'

She was a perennial girl of summer – blonde, big boned, tanned since birth. Had this been the American midwest, she would have been a one-time cheerleader – a straw-haired, seriously uncomplicated epitome of wholesome New Worldliness. As this was the antipodean sector of the New World, however, wholesomeness didn't figure in her make-up. Rather, she came across as one of those women who knew a thing or two about handling a surfboard and also about handling herself in a culture which takes pride in its inherent maleness, its self-conscious virility. And, as this was the trading floor of a major bank, her beach-bum demeanour was toned down by a floral print dress and a string of pearls.

'You don't want to speak to me,' Jane Howard said after Johnno introduced us. 'I mean, I know sweet F.A. about the way things work here. I've only been with this bank for seven days.'

'Seven *days*?' I said. 'You're joking.'

'I'm serious,' she said, and explained that she'd only joined Johnno's team last week. Before then, she'd spent a year in the money markets division of a rival bank. And, directly before that job, she'd been a nurse on a sheep station in the Northern Territory.

'A year ago at this time, I was bandaging up blokes after fights. Now I'm trading D-marks in bloody Sydney. Twelve months ago, if you'd've asked me what a D-mark was, I would've probably said it was some fancy boutique beer.'

'What got you out of that sheep station?' I asked.

'My fella. He got tired of selling insurance in Woop-Woop, so he upped and came down here. Got a job in the money markets within two months. I was presented with a rather basic choice – either I stayed a nurse up in the Territory, continued to make do with $13,000 a year, and forgot about seeing this bloke again, or I gave it all up and joined him in the Smoke.'

She paused for a moment and gave me one of those deliberate looks that is crammed with irony. 'It was the money that decided me,' she said. 'Especially when the bastard told me he was making 40k a year.'

So Jane came down to the big golden city, hitting Sydney in the midst of a boom market – which meant it wasn't that difficult to make the transition from nursing to Forex, as there were plenty of jobs going in the trading sector. And now, a mere twelve months after storming into town, she'd found her way to the floor of the sexiest trading room in Sydney.

I met Jane in a small lounge off the trading floor during one of her smokos – a coffee and cigarette break. She didn't smoke, but she was obviously something of a caffeine junkie, as she chain-drank four cups of toxic office java while we chatted. Two young women entered the lounge and Jane called them over.

'Meet Liz and Arabella,' she said. 'My partners in crime.'

They were both twenty-two years old – new recruits to the trading floor from the University of Sydney. Arabella was one of those anorexically thin women who favours angular suits with linebacker-style shoulderpads. Liz, on the other hand, was a future senior executive type – pinstriped, designer hornrimmed, armed with a technospeak vocabulary.

'You know what they call us in Sydney?' Liz said. 'The lifestyle bank. And the reason why is because our corporate culture here is high profile: big money, big perks.'

'You name a restaurant in Sydney, we've eaten in it,' Arabella said.

'Yeah,' Liz said, 'and you've never picked up a tab.'

Arabella gave Liz a challenging smile. Then, turning to me, she said, 'You should've seen Liz when she first got on the floor. She actually thought the whole world was Catholic. Still does.'

'These two slag each other all day,' Jane said. 'They think it keeps them competitive.'

'One week here,' Liz said, 'and she's already the bloody floor psychologist . . . or should I say nurse?'

'Are coffee breaks always like this?' I asked.

'Usually worse,' Arabella said.

'Especially if there are blokes around,' Liz said.

'The floor must be rather bloke-orientated,' I said.

'*Rather* bloke-orientated?' Arabella said. 'This place is *totally* bloke-orientated.'

'And when we say "bloke-orientated",' Liz said, 'we mean seriously rough. I mean, when I first started at the Forex desk, the jokes went right over my head . . . '

'Like a good little Catholic girl . . . ' Arabella said.

' . . . but now,' Liz continued, 'if I hear a joke and it's not crude, I wonder if it's a joke in the first place. Life on the floor really toughens you up.'

I asked the trio if they ever got nervous about dealing in so much money.

'It doesn't seem like money,' Jane said, 'which means that it all becomes an abstraction. I mean, at first you're really awed by the figures, but then you just get used to dealing in large sums. It gets a little strange, though. Like, just the other day I was scribbling out a cheque which was supposed to be for one hundred dollars, but I accidentally wrote "One Million" instead, because that's the sort of figure I deal with all the time.'

Liz said, 'You really don't think too much about the risk factor. You're more concerned about the margin of error that's involved. Because it's a very precise game that you're playing. And very, very competitive.'

'How competitive?' I asked.

'Everybody wants to be number one,' Arabella said. 'Everybody wants to be the profit centre of the desk they work. Because they know they can get the sack tomorrow. That's the hardest thing about this place – it demands everything from you, but you know you can't get too emotionally or financially tied to it, since you might not be working here next week. And realizing that always makes you uneasy.'

I asked Jane if she too was acquainted with that unease.

'The way I see it, Sydney's nothing but one big mining town. You come down here to make your stake, you hopefully hit it big, and then you get out. I mean, when I'm thirty-five, I hope to be living in the suburbs, having kids and playing tennis. The only thing I want to get out of my time here is a bit of financial independence – which, for a woman, is an important thing. So I refuse to get too stressed about life on the floor. I mean, I don't want to have a heart attack.'

'Like poor old George,' Liz said.

'Yeah,' Arabella said. 'That was sad.'

'Who was George?' I asked.

'One of our traders,' Liz said.

'Had a coronary,' Arabella said. 'Had to give up the floor.'

'And he was only twenty-seven,' Liz said.

'What brought it on?' I asked.

'A big overnight move in Deutschmarks,' Liz said.

Sydney as mining town. The City of Gold, waiting to be plundered. It was an apt analogy. And, like any place where nuggets had been unearthed, it was teeming with prospectors hoping to strike a profitable vein which would set them up for life.

Of course, all big cities are ultimately mining towns, with the promise of bottomless lodes beneath their surface. But Sydney's financial markets really did embrace the Gold Rush spirit – especially as many of those digging for riches knew they would never survive a long stint down the mines. Listening to Jane, Liz and Arabella, what struck me most forcibly was their cheerful fatalism; their acceptance of the fact that this really was their five minutes in the sun, that they had a sell-by date posted over their heads.

What a curious way to pass one's twenties – in a highly

remunerative job with a limited lifespan, and with no future prospects after you crossed the threshold of your thirtieth birthday. It was almost as if you were guaranteeing yourself a premature midlife crisis when you found yourself off the trading floor and were faced with the little question of what you were going to do for the rest of your life. No wonder so many traders thrived on the self-validation aspects of the marketplace, and were in such a hurry to achieve so much so fast. If you knew that, professionally speaking, you were living on borrowed time, wouldn't you grab as much as you could from your stint on the floor? In the 1980s aggressive, rapacious young traders were regarded as embodying a 'greed is good' ethic. But wasn't their supposed greed a natural response to such an environment? And, if it was avarice that made them work fourteen-hour days in a financial snakepit, why did so many of them downshift into thoroughly unambitious occupations after their final departure from the floor? Was the competitive instinct bled out of them after a decade of shouting down a phone line? Or had they always craved something unambitious in the first place? Was greed a means to a mundane end? Did they put in ten frantic years in order to finance an unstressful existence peddling bottles of Cabernet Sauvignon? Or did their post-marketplace need for the mundane arise out of a sense of fear? A fear born of the knowledge that life on the floor was ultimately dangerous to their health. Especially when it came to a bad movement of Deutschmarks.

It was like gaining entrance to a casino. A high-security casino which catered to the sort of high rollers who actually needed high security. Its discreet entrance was tucked away in a crevasse of an office block – a narrow gash in the reinforced concrete. When you reached it, you were met by a mass of security apparatus – closed-circuit cameras; electronic turnstiles; metal detectors; a trio of heavies manning a bank of monitors and phones, and politely interrogating any non-regulars who approached its threshold.

It was easy to tell who was a regular player in this joint, as they were decked out in an array of zoot suit jackets – all screaming orange checks and pink polkadots and lime green swirls. The sort of jackets that are usually associated with the Surrealists of the 1920s, or with Bozo the Clown. If you weren't wearing one of these caterwauling jackets and didn't have a pass card for the turnstiles, you weren't going to get further than the front door without being asked to state your business. If you wanted to visit the playing floor, security was even tighter. You had to be invited by a registered 'croupier', who had to inform security of your intended call at least twenty-four hours in advance. And when you showed up, you were temporarily relieved of your briefcase, invited to step through a metal detector, and then pin a visitor's badge to your breast. Only when your host appeared downstairs at security were you permitted to step through the electronic turnstiles and finally gain access to the Sydney Futures Exchange.

My host was called Wendy. A petite woman nearing the benchmark of middle age, with a tired but easy smile. When we first met (over dinner at a friend's house in Sydney), her waif-like demeanour and the tight collection of blonde curls framing her head put me in mind of a silent-film actress – Mary Pickford? There was still a strong hint of Merseyside in her voice ten years after her emigration to *Terra Australis*. Given her wide-eyed countenance, it was a little bemusing to hear her spout on about bank bills, ten-year bonds and her work as a white-badge trader on the exchange floor. When she offered me the chance to see the exchange in action, I immediately made a date with her for the following week.

'Sorry about the security,' Wendy said as she came down the stairs from the trading floor. 'But they don't take any chances around here. Especially since it would only take one wanker mingling on the floor to send the entire market into bloody chaos.'

'Love the jacket,' I said, taking in the riotous purple-blotched number she wore over her suit.

'Yeah, it's beaut,' Wendy said. 'An original Karl Lagerfeld.'

Above us came the sort of roar that wouldn't have been out of place at a Cup Final. As we climbed the stairs, this clamour of voices intensified, to the point where I actually began to feel as if we were about to walk into the centre of a vast, packed amphitheatre. Instead, we pushed through a set of swing doors and became part of an expertly choreographed imbroglio.

Having loitered in assorted bourses and dealing rooms over the past few months, I was well used to the cacophony of traders at work. But nothing I'd encountered to date really prepared me for the jet-propelled chaos of the Sydney Futures Exchange. Passing through those swing doors was like plunging into a souk on dexedrine, a place where buying and selling was a high-velocity activity. The soundtrack of the Exchange was one of hellbent babble – speculative commerce at 78 rpm. As I took in the throng of dealers encircling the small trading pits with electronic monitors suspended overhead, the casino image took root once again. Walk into a gambling joint in Monte Carlo, Atlantic City, Vegas or Reno, and you'll see clusters of players decked out in more expensive variations of the same wow-'em jackets huddling around the craps, blackjack and roulette tables. Here you saw similar congregations of gamblers, only the *jeux de chance* on offer happened to be things like ninety-day bank bills, Australian and American dollars, treasury bonds, gold, and even live cattle. Because it was a futures exchange, the speculative game everyone was playing had to do with buying or selling a standard quantity of a commodity on a specific future date at an agreed price that was being determined now, in this open marketplace.

In other words, the brokers in the pits were fixing a price today for something their clients wanted in the future. And the trading method they used to shout their bids and offers was called open outcry.

Open outcry. There was something quasi-operatic, quasi-psychodramatic about that expression. Then again, the Futures Exchange was a sort of operatic psychodrama, abrim with overblown theatrical gestures and emotional ventilation. After pushing me onto a small viewing platform, Wendy re-entered the pits and immediately began to scream. In fact, she appeared to be attempting a curious feat: screaming and speaking in sign language at the same time. As she joined the chorus of bellowing pit dealers and then shouted for the attention of one of her colleagues manning a group of phones facing the pit, she was also conveying trading information to him through an extraordinarily complex array of hand signals. First she made a 'come here' motion with her right hand. Then that hand shot upwards. Then it touched her forehead. Then it made the sort of sweeping off-the-chin motion which, in Italy, usually means *Va a fa'n culo.* Later, Wendy gave me a crash course in the gestural vocabulary of futures trading. The 'come here' motion means 'I want to buy,' whereas holding your hand up like a policeman ordering someone to stop indicates that you want to sell. Holding up your fingers indicates the numbers one to five, and the numbers six to nine are signalled by gesturing to the side with the same fingers. A clenched fist is a zero. Counting in tens is achieved by touching your forehead, while the hand motion under the chin denotes the number of units of a commodity you want to buy or sell.

So, say a dealer in the ninety-day bank bills pits made a stop motion with his right hand, then ricocheted two fingers off his forehead, then pointed upwards with four fingers, then closed his fist, the gist of his message would be 'I sell twenty at forty.' If he found himself in trouble over a transaction, he'd poke his middle finger up in the air, then make as if he was cutting his throat with it. Translation: 'Help me, I'm fucked.'

There were gestures denoting the different companies operating in the pits, and others signifying every broker as well (Wendy told me she was symbolized by a pair of impatiently snapping fingers, as she was known to be restless. She also said – with a certain amount of pride – that if your fellow dealers hadn't thought up a sign for you, you could consider yourself a nobody on the floor).

In addition to this intricate glossary of gestures, there was also an entire dealership hierarchy to contend with. Like the military, one's rank in this hierarchy was indicated by the sort of badge or stripe you wore on your uniform. Wendy, for example, was a white-badge trader. This meant she was the most senior class of broker in the pit, with full trading rights, and could deal in any commodity she wanted without supervision. Directly below her were the yellow-badge traders – trainee brokers under the supervision of a white-badger. Then there were market clerks who wore red badges and had no trading rights, but played an administrative role in all the dealing activity. Finally there were the blue-badged 'locals', the freelancers of the exchange, either trading with their own money or on behalf of another floor broker.

White, yellow, red and blue badges. Wildly coloured jackets denoting corporate affiliation. And a language which only insiders could understand. Entering the Futures Exchange was like entering a foreign country. And perhaps the most extraordinary feature of this society was the way in which traders like Wendy could effortlessly cross the border back into normalcy after three hours of open outcry. When the bell rang signalling the end of the morning trading session, and the roar of the trading floor was suddenly stilled, and Wendy traded her purple-blotched dealing jacket for something off-white and linen, I expected her to be panting for breath the way a long-distance runner does after a race. Instead, she had the composed look of someone who thought nothing of standing in a pit and roaring for 180 straight minutes.

Sidling up to me in the visitors' gallery, she said, 'Not a bad morning's work. Lunch?'

We walked over to The Rocks, the oldest part of Sydney, built with convict labour. Now it was a gentrified, theme-parkish sort of district: tourist shops, cappuccino cafés and hi-tech bars brimming with designer people. Wendy guided me to an open-air restaurant in the shadow of the Harbour Bridge. Sitting there, under a hard, cobalt blue sky, with the sweep of the harbour in front of us and the high-rise mercantile wall of the central business district defining the eastern and southern horizons, the romance of Sydney as a playpen of ambition asserted itself once again. I asked Wendy if her first sight of this cityscape had fuelled her aspirations. She barked a bleak laugh.

'When I first arrived here, I was a twenty-one-year-old wife of a plumber. My only ambition was a house in the Western suburbs with purple net curtains. All this . . . ' her hand followed the curve of the harbour ' . . . was completely unreal to me. Especially since I almost never came into the city from the Westies.'

Ending up in Australia itself had been something of a fluke. Wendy was a Kirby girl, and had hardly been outside Liverpool and environs when she saw an advertisement in the *Observer* one Sunday in 1975 about emigration to Oz. She'd been married for three years to Keith, whom she'd met and become engaged to at school. Although they were both gainfully employed – he installing central heating with a big plumbing concern, she working as a clerk in the DHSS – the grim realities of seventies Britain had left them both feeling doubtful about the future state of the nation. So Wendy clipped the coupon and despatched it to Australia House in The Strand. A questionnaire arrived a week later. Wendy filled it out and tossed it into a postbox, and was surprised to receive word from the Australian Department of Migration and Ethnic Affairs that there was a shortage of skilled plumbers in New South Wales. Before Wendy and Keith knew it, they'd been given the all-clear by the Australian authorities, had closed down their lives in Kirby and had taken wing to Sydney in possession of a suitcase each and a box of Keith's plumbing implements – as the migration certificate informed Keith that he was allowed to bring the tools of his trade *and* his spouse.

Within seventy-two hours of their arrival in Sydney, a still jet-lagged Keith walked into a job. Twenty-four hours later, Wendy also had employment, as a bookkeeper in a medical supply company, and had signed on to do a night-time business studies course at a local college. By the end of their first week they were ensconced in a rented house in the Westies, and fully convinced that they had landed in some magic kingdom where everything was possible.

For Wendy, at least, the magic continued. Six months later she switched jobs, getting an administrative post with a company that traded in the metals market. She was walking down a corridor on her first day on the job when she ran into an executive who had been on her interview panel.

'Oh, hello again,' he said. 'You wouldn't happen to know what "futures" are, would you?'

Wendy acknowledged that she'd heard the word, and was, in fact, studying the workings of the Futures Exchange in her night classes. The man seemed impressed, and asked her another question.

'Can you shout loudly?'

Wendy nodded.

'Follow me,' he said. Wendy followed him out of the office and across the city to the Futures Exchange, and never looked back. Why had she been plucked from the doldrums of clerk-dom and transplanted to the razzle-dazzle of the marketplace? As she later found out, gold had jumped by $10 on the day she started her new job, and when she ran into her former interviewer in the corridor he was on the prowl for someone to be a 'booth mole', which essentially meant manning the phones in a small cubicle on the Exchange floor (the job also requires a resilient set of vocal chords, as the booth mole has to shout above the chaos going on all around). Wendy worked the phones for a year – relaying and filing orders, making certain that traders never oversold, learning the business of buying and selling futures, and discovering that she herself, the plumber's wife from Kirby, might just have a future as the first woman trader on the floor of the Sydney Exchange.

'Becoming the first woman to shout on the Exchange got to be an obsession of mine,' Wendy said. 'I went to my boss, who told me he'd previously auditioned two other women as yellow-badge traders, and both of them had ended up crying in the Australian dollar pit. In other words, he didn't think women had the stamina it takes to trade futures. I kept having to cajole the bastard into giving me a shot. It took three months, but finally he got so bloody sick of me asking him for a chance to wear a yellow badge that he gave in. But first he had to get permission from the directors of the company before he could let me go into the pits. Then he told all the other traders that the only reason I was being given a chance as a yellow-badger was to "keep the skirt in the company happy". What's more, the little bugger also laid 6-1 odds that I wouldn't survive more than a fortnight in the pit. I'll tell you something: that bloke might've given me my break on the floor, but he's just like every other Australian man I've ever met – behaves like a rug rat.' It took a day or two of asking around, but I finally learned that a rug rat was an Australian expression for a two-year-old child.

Wendy's rug rat boss was seriously surprised when Sydney's first woman futures trader not only survived her first fortnight in the pits, but went on to earn her white badge within six months.

'I was the hot new kid on the block, and I knew it. Futures and me were like love at first sight. And as far as I was concerned, the Exchange was the most important place in the world – because, let's face it, it pulled me out of being a bookkeeper, a clerk, and gave me $80,000 a year, when I used to make $16,000. When you grow up in Kirby, you don't think about making 80k a year. I mean, that was the hardest thing for me about becoming a white-badger – convincing myself that I was actually worth eighty thousand bloody bucks a year.'

She paused for a moment to ignite a cigarette, her Zippo lighter opening and closing with an emphatic crack.

'No, I lie,' she said. 'The hardest thing about becoming a white-badger was watching my marriage fall apart. Because futures killed it. Killed it stone dead.'

The trouble started as soon as Wendy got her first break in the pits. With all her male colleagues laying book that she wouldn't survive as a trader, she was putting in fourteen-hour days to ensure that 'the bastards wouldn't win a penny off my predicted failure'. Keith found himself coming home to an empty house every night, and getting phone calls from Wendy at around 9 p.m. promising she'd make it back by midnight. This did not go down well with a bloke who expected his dinner on the table after he got home from a long day of clearing blocked drains. Eventually he demanded that Wendy give up her job and return to a nine-to-five routine.

This was a strategic mistake. If Wendy did give up her fledgling career as a futures trader, she'd resent Keith for the rest of her life. And if he failed to talk her back into the kitchen the marriage would still be hopelessly snookered, since he'd become even more embittered about coming home to an empty house and a dinnerless dining table. Keith had essentially handed Wendy an ultimatum: 'Choose the markets or me.' In doing so, he'd forgotten that ultimatums are the Russian roulette of marriage – issue one, and you take a gamble that it might just blow the alliance away.

'The last thing I wanted was to see my marriage collapse. But despite the fact that we went to counselling, Keith was still adamant that I either stay with him or stay with futures. He just wouldn't compromise on the subject. Know why? Because he simply couldn't handle the idea that I was making almost three times as much money as him. He actually equated me pulling down 80k with me kneeing him in his pride.'

Inevitably, the centre did not hold and things between Wendy and Keith fell apart. She moved out, exchanging suburbia for a flat with a cinemascope view of the waters of the golden city. Although she suffered from a long bout of the blues after the divorce came through, she had her work as an antidote. Seven years on, she was now one of the top futures traders in town (not to mention one of the most senior, as she'd beaten the odds and was still a dealer in her mid-thirties). She was still living alone in the same panoramic flat, still using work as a means of deflecting her gloom.

'I'm an extrovert, I suppose, which is why I like trading. And there's nothing like a fifteen-hour day to make you forget the fact that you don't have any personal life to speak of. Then again, you need to be obsessive when it comes to trading futures. It really does take a certain temperament. Probably the hardest thing to learn is how to let go of anger. Like, if you've had a shitty day and dropped a bundle, you simply have to dismiss what's happened and move on. Otherwise you go berserk. I mean, I had a young bloke working for me as a yellow-badger who simply couldn't handle the pressure. One day he turned around and put his fist through a board.'

'A bulletin board?' I asked.

'An electronic board. Ten k's worth of technology. Now he's working as a lifeguard in Queensland.

'And I kind of envy him, up there on the beach. Especially since I'm way beyond the usual age for a pit dealer. And I know I'm going to have to make a move in a few years. But what scares me most is this: I don't know what else to do any more. I mean, where am I going to find another job that pays me eighty thousand to scream all day?'

On Fridays, after the last bell has sounded, the dealers of the Sydney Futures Exchange repair to the bar of the Hotel Inter-Continental and begin the process of drowning the tensions of the trading week. Schooners of beer arrive on large trays and are tossed down with breathtaking rapidity. Within minutes of their arrival, most dealers have drained three large glasses with the 'I've been dreaming of this' intensity of someone who's been crawling through the desert for days.

The dealers are out of uniform. The hallucinatory jackets have been put away for the weekend, and everyone is dressed in civvies – dark suits for men and women alike.

'The team is off the field,' Wendy says, ordering up another round. The place is packed – a phalanx of navy blue and grey pinstripe and prematurely thickening necks. Look closely at the way the crowd is grouped, however, and you'll notice that the team analogy is an apt one, for everyone is socializing exclusively with members of their own division from the trading floor. Officers here; foot soldiers there.

'We white-badgers tend to hang out together,' Ken tells me. He's one of Wendy's colleagues, aged around twenty-five, from Queensland; a muscular testament to the wonders of antipodean dentistry and ultra-violet rays.

'Being a dealer makes you a bit schizoid. I mean, when you're on the floor you have to behave like an outrageous arsehole. And then when you get off the floor, you revert to type . . . which also means that you behave like an outrageous arsehole, only you're a little more relaxed about it. But, y'know, before I went to futures I was in a trading room. And believe me, a trading room can get far more intense than a pit – especially if you have a big movement taking place. Still, there's really nothing like a pit for getting the adrenalin working on overdrive. And if I step off the floor for a five-minute break and then suddenly hear that . . . *roar* behind me . . . Christ, that roar is something else. Most seductive bloody sound I know. 'Cause it's a sound that tells you – Son, you really are in the centre of things.

'And, yeah, you really do have to have a certain mentality to work the pits. You've got to be the kind of bloke who, when the ship is going down, won't think twice about fighting for a place in the lifeboat. You can be a perfect gentleman off the floor; on it, it's that old cliché about survival of the fittest.'

I asked Ken what was the hardest thing about working the pits. 'The stress,' he said. And the best thing about the pits? 'The stress,' he said again.

Phil agreed with Ken – knowing how to cope with the frenzied perturbations of the marketplace was crucial to the professional survival of all futures traders. Phil was another white-badger, a far more hardened-looking variation on the boy-of-summer theme. The kind of sinewy, pit-bullish, battle-hardened type you could easily imagine browsing through the pages of *Soldier of Fortune*, wondering if Angola was still in the market for his services. If Ken was the beachcomber, then Phil was the lifeguard.

'You know why so many dealers in Sydney live by the beach?' Phil asked. 'Two reasons. One, because being able to afford a place by the water is kind of a pay-off for doing such a crazy bloody job; and two, because at the end of a real mind-fuck day, being able to sit out on your balcony with a couple of cold ones, staring at the surf, tends to put everything in perspective. And if you can't find an apartment by the beach, you get a place with a pool. As long as you have proximity to water, you should keep your equilibrium on the floor.'

Proximity to water – the great fringe benefit of a Sydney futures dealer. A high-priced safety valve affording you easy access to the tranquillizing benefits of sun and surf. There was something curiously vulnerable about Phil's admission that a beachfront view gave him the illusion that, beyond the merciless rivalry of the floor, he was still somehow connected to the insouciant world of the endless Australian summer. There was also something intriguing about the fact that Phil and Ken quizzed me about which contemporary Australian writers I'd read, and seemed to know their stuff when it came to discussing the state of fiction in their country today. Then again, I hadn't encountered a single dealer who conformed to the 'Lemme tell you about the size of my Porsche and my penis' image of the identikit philistine trader. That is, until I met Jerry Brilliant.

'Why you talking to these fuckheads? You wanna know about life on the floor, you gotta talk to me.'

An American, around thirty, with a middle-aged girth and babyfat cheeks, Jerry was a white-badger doing a three-year stint as Our Man in Sydney for a big L.A. commodities group. He may have been an Angeleno, but he dressed like an old-style Chicago ward boss: silver Diamond Jim suit, white-on-white shirt, chunky opal cufflinks and a silver tie. A pair of rimless spectacles shielded his eyes. There was something vaguely menacing about those specs. They hinted at a clinical ruthlessness lurking within the robber baron suit, and behind the voice that gatecrashed our conversation with all the subtlety of an articulated lorry.

'Lemme tell you something 'bout these guys,' Jerry said. 'They all tell themselves, "I'll get out when I have enough money." Open some goddamn newspaper shop or some kinda fucking liquor store. Isn't that right, Phil baby?'

Phil said nothing; he simply looked into his beer.

'Scratch all of these guys and you'll find . . . the dream. The quiet, shitbrain life away from the market. Well, I say: Fuck all that. 'Cause as far as I'm concerned, everyone knows what this job's about – it's about putting your dick on the chopping block every day and hoping you ain't separated from it by nightfall. That is why they pay you such big do-re-mi – 'cause you're risking your schlong. So why complain? This is your job. This is how you live. This is what you *do*. And what the fuck is wrong with that?'

'Jerry talks a loud game,' Wendy said as we left the Inter, 'but around his wife he's like a ten-year-old kid. Then again, she is one big lady. I mean, we're talking seriously large. And she knows how to handle him. You should see Jerry in the pub when he's ringing home and can't get through. He comes back to us, all nervous, saying stuff like, "Okay, you saw me trying to ring home, so you'll vouch for me, right?" He's genuinely scared of her because I think he's also terrified of losing her – which is usually how it works, isn't it?'

I asked Wendy whether many Australians considered Jerry an acquired taste.

'See that pub over there,' she said, pointing across the street to the entrance of an *ersatz* Victorian saloon. 'Jerry got beaten up in there last month.'

'How'd he manage to do that?'

'He started hassling a guy who was playing one of those poker machines. Telling him he didn't know jack shit about five-card draw and he should let him have a go. Now, to give the bloke his due, he did keep telling Jerry to lay off, but Jerry simply never knows when to lay off. You should see him in a restaurant – always screaming at the waitress, always sending his food back. And he's a wine snob to boot. Anyway . . . this bloke in the pub lost another hand of poker on the machine, and Jerry started making comments about his lack of intelligence, saying stuff like, "Don't pick your nose or your head'll cave in." Which is when the bloke lost it completely and essentially rearranged Jerry's face. We had to rush the dumb bastard to the hospital. Two stitches in his lip, three below the left eye.

'Still, the people in the Exchange put up with Jerry because he's such an excellent trader. Really knows his stuff and he's very, very profitable. Which is why he's still alive in this business.'

We walked across the after-hours streets of the central business district. Shuttered office blocks, the occasional pool of street light, the onset of the weekend. Except for one public square where a hundred or so suits stood drinking in the night air.

'That's the Customs House Bar,' Wendy said. 'The second biggest "market" bar in town. Look at them. They're probably telling each other what a fantastic day they all had. How much money they made. In other words, lying to each other. And I'll let you in on a little secret. Half of those people are probably going to be out of a job within the next year. Because the boom economy has well and truly pegged out. Every trading house in town is looking at reduced profit margins, which means that they're going to start making economies by cutting off the heads of as many dealers as they can get away with. I tell you, mate – you came to Sydney just in time to see the end of the party. Not that anyone's talking about the party being over – that would mean owning up to bad news. And if there's one thing traders can't handle, it's admitting that they're in some kind of jeopardy. You have to keep up the illusion that you're on a constant winning streak in this game. You have to bullshit everyone. You even have to bullshit yourself.'

There was one other major centre of human activity in the darkened central business district. It was called Syd's: a bar tucked beneath an office block, with a concrete piazza out front for *al fresco* drinking. The joint was packed, the jukebox was pumping out deafening disco funk, the average age of the clientele was around twenty-four.

'All dealers,' Wendy shouted over the din. 'The Customs House is where they come to talk business and get laid. Or at least try to get laid.'

We battled our way to the bar, where glasses of local champagne were five dollars a throw. On the way back to the piazza we ran into another of Wendy's white-badge colleagues, Neil. He gave her a big wet kiss, and then accidentally baptized his speckled suit with the contents of his champagne glass. The fizzy liquid congealed with the cigarette ash already on his jacket.

'Had a little to drink?' Wendy asked him.

Neil made an affectionate lunge for her, attempting to stick his tongue down her throat. To fend off his attack, Wendy told him that I was writing a book about the marketplace. Immediately, in true pub bore fashion, Neil had me cornered.

'You wanna know about the market? I'll tell you about the market. The market's shit. And I'm getting out.'

Neil then proceeded to give me the large print edition of his life story – how his old man was a brickie, and how upset he was when Neil wouldn't follow him into the trade but found himself a job at the age of sixteen (courtesy of the Commonwealth Employment Service) as a runner on the floor of the Futures Exchange. A lucky break here, a lucky break there, and, hey presto . . . Neil was a yellow-badger at the age of nineteen, graduating to white-badge status two years later.

'I've been a white-badger for four years now, and I'm sick of it. The only reason I've stayed on is because they pay such fantastic salaries, and it's given me the opportunity to make some big money at an early age. But around twelve months ago I came to the conclusion that what I was doing didn't really do anybody any good; that I'd rather be doing something constructive. Y'know what the market's about? Killing yourself on the floor so you can have a good time afterwards. That's why everyone's here tonight . . . to have a good time. I'm fucking tired of having a good time. I want to . . .'

'Do something constructive?' I asked.

'Yeah. Help humanity. That kinda shit.'

I pressed him on the issue. After nearly a decade in futures, he must have something good to say about it. He thought about this one for a moment.

'When the floor's busy,' he finally said, 'and you've got work to do, it's very exciting and you make a lot of money. But who cares about making money if you don't believe in what you're doing? If you think you work in a meaningless industry?'

'Don't you think you're being a little simplistic?'

'You calling me simple?' Neil said, suddenly dangerous.

I assured Neil that I wasn't questioning his intelligence – only his reasons for quitting his job.

'I'm quitting my job . . . because I'm interested in learning.'

'Learning about what?' I asked.

'About life.'

'Isn't the floor life?'

'The floor isn't the real world. I mean, how can it be when I make three times as much as a university professor – and I'm only twenty-five. How can that be real?'

'Sounds real enough to me,' I said.

We were interrupted by the arrival of a young woman. Heavy make-up. Tight dress. Tight blouse. Badly dyed blonde hair. Loud voice. Very drunk. Name of Cassie. A stockbroker.

101

'Are you a client of his?' she asked me.

'No.'

'Then why're you taking notes?'

'It's a habit of mine,' I said.

'What you taking notes about?'

'Me leaving the market,' Neil said.

'Why you leaving the market?'

'Because it's bullshit.'

'Everything's bullshit.'

'I just don't like what I'm doing.'

'Maybe you're not happy with the people you work with on the floor,' she said.

'It's not that . . . '

'Then what's brassing you off?'

'I'm not doing anything constructive.'

'What's your idea of constructive?'

'Healing.'

'Healing?'

'I want to be a healer,' Neil said. 'Do a massage course after I leave futures. Get into alternative medicine. Stuff like that.'

'And you call the market bullshit?' she said, and then did an about-face, turning her back on Neil.

'Hey, Gordie,' she shouted to a beefy guy with a mop of blond hair, 'buy me another glass of fizz.'

'Bitch,' Neil said *sotto voce*. 'Her idea of constructiveness is lying on her back spreading her legs.'

'Don't you think she had a point?' I asked.

There was a long pause. Then Neil said: 'See that car park across the street. That used to be a building. A building with a couple of shops. They tore it down. That used to be a place, understand? A *place*. But now it's a fucking car park. D'you see what happens when money wants something? D'you see what I'm getting at?'

Then he walked away. And it struck me that the saddest sort of idealist is one who has yet to figure out what he should be idealistic about. Especially after six years as a trader on the floor of the Sydney Futures Exchange.

Later that night, as we were polishing off a second bottle of semillon in a wine bar, Wendy said: 'My problem is that I'm treated like a guy by the guys on the floor. They like me because I can act like a bloke towards them – which means that they respect me as a trader, but wouldn't look at me as a woman. I watch them watching other women, and I see that they see me as just another dealer.'

We were both seriously oiled, but Wendy still insisted on ordering a third bottle. As she splashed a little more of the yellow wine into her glass, she said: 'You know, I had an affair for a year with a trader on the floor. He was married, of course. Which means that it ended predictably.'

'Does he still work at the Exchange?' I asked.

'Yeah. I see him every day.'

'How do you handle it?'

'I outbid the bastard.'

'Want to hear a funny paradox?' Trevor Thompson asked. 'All my life I dreamed about living next to the water. In fact, I think one of the reasons I ended up in the markets was because I knew it would finance a place with a harbour view. Now I've got the house by the water, but no job in the markets. You know what the moral of the story is? Water fucks you up in Sydney.'

Water. The more I lingered on, the more I felt that water was the key to understanding Sydney. Water defined the city, giving it an effervescent sheen. And water also defined your status within the metropolis. To live in a choice suburban inlet like Double Bay or Mosman, or up on the northern beaches near the Bilgola Bends, was an acknowledgment that you were a member of the higher echelons of Australian life. Water in Sydney embodied the country's golden promise of a sweet life. No wonder so many dealers craved 'proximity to water'. A seafront dwelling wasn't simply a badge of status;

it was also, in many ways, the ultimate realization of a deeply Australian, deeply hedonistic dream – laid-back, sun-dappled prosperity. Though Australians liked to boast that theirs was a supremely informal society, lurking behind the good-blokish conviviality was the determined ruthlessness inherent in all New World cultures where people didn't 'know their place'; where everything was up for grabs. And in Sydney, a city of hustlers, you wheeled and dealed and gutted the competition in order to get to the water.

But what happened once you'd made it to the water? What happened if, like Trevor Thompson, you finally arrived there after twenty years of struggle and were then suddenly dropped from active service in the markets?

'What happened when they sacked me?' Trevor Thompson said. 'I came back home and thought, "Fuck me – I'm walking the wallaby track."'

Walking the wallaby track is Australian for finding yourself on the road to nowhere. Trevor's wallaby track had brought him to this hardwood deck in Mosman overlooking an inlet of Sydney Harbour. By day, Mosman was an antipodean variation on a Côte d'Azur theme – a cluster of sunstruck Mediterranean houses and pleasure boats curving across a squat finger of water. By night, with the sloshing waters of the harbour illuminated by the spectral light of a full moon, and a set of wind chimes counterpointing this aquatic metronome, it was the pinnacle of antipodean romance. Trevor Thompson – a paunchy, tired man in an Armani tracksuit – sat in a deckchair extracting the cork from the fourth bottle of Hunter Valley chardonnay. His wife Roz, a stockbroker, cleared up the remnants of our Thai take-aways and said goodnight. Trevor and I toasted each other as midnight ushered in another day in the land of midnight money. Then he got talking about the state of the country, and the Utopian bubble burst. 'The Australian fascination with money has always been huge. That's because this country has always had a lot of money – a lot more than most outsiders would give it credit for. And the fascination is with who's the richest and how much money they've got. There's a business magazine in Sydney which publishes a weekly list of the richest people and richest companies in the country. Everybody I know turns to that list first thing every week to see who's up and who's down. Because high finance in this country is like following the racing game or the pop charts. It's all sport. And sport needs its heroes. Which is why, in the mid-eighties, the public was absolutely gripped by the exploits of the Bonds and the Packers and the Holmes à Courts – because they were seen to be going out into the world and conquering it. And it gave Australians a certain pride to see their entrepreneurs making it so big. But, like I said, the pride was all caught up with the idea of winning. As soon as the big boys started getting into trouble, or starting dropping dead from heart attacks like Holmes à Court, public opinion turned right against them, because they weren't winners anymore.

'But now, the thing of it is, none of us are winners any more. It's like the entire Australian population is waking up from a collective forty-year binge with the biggest financial hangover imaginable. I mean, up until a year or two ago, we always thought stuff like double-digit unemployment, double-digit inflation, double-digit interest rates were Pommy diseases we were immune to. Now we're finding out that we're as susceptible to economic downturn as anyone else. Sometimes I think we're like a bloke who spent years and years happily screwing every sheila he stumbled across, and then woke up one morning to discover that not only was he being hit with thirty-five paternity suits, he also had an irreversible case of the clap to boot.'

I asked Trev if he too had been deluded by the binge mentality of the past few decades.

'Well, that's kinda bloody obvious, innit? I mean, I hit Sydney in 1968, fresh out of uni in Adelaide – a parochial kid who knew fuck all about anything. And I spent the next twenty-odd years getting paid scandalous amounts of money for doing something that really doesn't take much in the way of heavyweight intellectual brainpower. Like, I'm sure you've probably heard a lot of mythological bullshit about how the ability to trade is some God-given gift. Let me tell you something: the best trader I ever knew was a former criminal. And the reason he was so good was because he understood, more than anyone else I've ever met, the basic rule of trading: something is only worth what you sell it for. Understand that – and know how to add – and you can be a trader, believe me.

'The reason I was able to stay a trader for so long was because I kept on the move – going from company to company. Y'see, I've got a low level of concentration, which suited me fine in the marketplace, because a trader never moves from job to job in search of a new challenge; he always moves on in search of a new opportunity. So, for two decades I kept cashing in on opportunities – and since I understood the basic rule of trading, and also only stayed with a company long enough to take what I could out of it, it was easy to be successful.

'But then, things began to contract around a year ago. And, for the first time in my professional life, I hit a bad patch. For almost four months, I lost money. I just couldn't get it right. Every deal I did, every position I took was a loser. And though I kept telling myself I'd turn the corner, somewhere deep down inside I knew that I just wasn't going to get out of the slump. Not for some time, anyway.

'Finally, my M.D. took me out to lunch. Spent most of the time talking about his home improvements, and as soon as the sweet showed up, he said, "I'm letting you go." Just like that. Twenty-two years as a profitable trader, and then a four-month slump gets you the sack. Not nice, eh? But par for the course. We play rough down here. Thing is, though, playing rough is fun when you're winning. When you're not . . . ' Trevor Thompson lifted the bottle and smiled a world-weary smile.

'I'll get back in. Just going to be a matter of time. Not that

I've had any tangible offers yet, what with the recession and all. But I'll be back. Or, at least, I keep telling myself that I'll be back. Got to keep the confidence up. I mean, when you're a trader, confidence is everything. 'Cause if you're not confident, you lose.'

We drank on till three – around which time Trevor tried to teach me a high-risk game which involved guessing the serial numbers on a $20 note. My brain was too fogged for such mathematical gambles, so I begged out, telling Trevor that I'd appreciate making the acquaintance of his spare bedroom.

'You're smart not to take me on,' Trevor said, the words slurring. ''Cause I would have played Australian-style.'

'What's Australian-style?' I asked.

'Letting you win a hand or two, and then taking you to the fucking cleaners.'

Four bottles of chardonnay had their predictable effect, and my overwrought bladder sent me a wake-up call three hours after I collapsed in Trevor's spare bedroom. I staggered off in search of a loo. After finding it, I made my way out to the deck, where Trevor was slumped in a deckchair, having failed to negotiate the corridor to his own bedroom. I stepped up to the railing and tried to focus on the water.

It was dark – a blackened canvas with only one small pinhole of light on the distant horizon. But soon the pinhole enlarged and lengthened and grew molten. Night woke up, the blackened sky parting at the middle to reveal the stern ferocity of the early morning sun.

As this harsh, incandescent sphere began to gain altitude, Trevor stirred out of his stupor, blinking madly in its glare. And said:

'Another fucking beautiful day in paradise.'

FIVE

The Faustian Bargain

The sign in the cubicle read:

IT IS AN OFFENCE NOT TO
FLUSH THE TOILET
Fine: $150

The toilet wouldn't flush, and I was a seriously worried man. I had heard the stories. The stories about the heat-sensor devices which the Singapore authorities had allegedly installed in every public commode, and which set off an alarm if the chain wasn't pulled. The stories about the flying squads of loo police who patrolled the toilets of this city-state, busting all those unhygienic, thoughtless and generally disgusting people who failed to flush away the aftermath of their bodily functions. Since the idea of a court appearance for such a pitiably squalid offence struck me as the ultimate in humiliation, I decided to report my predicament to a higher authority. His name was Mr Lee, and he was the manager of the hotel café where I was breakfasting. When I explained the problem, he immediately led me back to the scene of the crime and asked me to point out the cubicle in which the infraction of the sanitary laws had taken place. I did as requested. Mr Lee took down all the details of the incident in a little notebook, and asked for my room number in case the authorities needed my further help with their enquiries. Then, with a curt nod, he thanked me for my assistance in the matter, and for my social responsibility.

Social responsibility. I had been in Singapore for less than twenty-four hours, my brain was still tingling with jet-lag, and I was already falling into line. I was watching my step, following the rules, avoiding trouble. In short, I was behaving in a socially responsible fashion. Social responsibility – as I was rapidly discovering – was a sacred civic duty in Singapore.

Consider: after Mr Lee had finished his preliminary investigation into the unflushed toilet incident, I left the hotel and hopped a cab into the city centre. In New York, cab drivers either only speak Lithuanian or answer your request to take you north of 110th Street with pithy comments like, 'No way, asshole.' In Dublin, they welcome home returning residents at the airport with statements like, 'Don't know why yez bothered comin' back. The country's fucked.' And in London, they always seem to be engaged in stream-of-consciousness monologues that open with the line, 'So I told that wanker . . .'

In Singapore, on the other hand, the cab drivers practise social responsibility. A sign posted in the back of this immaculately valeted Toyota saloon informed me that I was in a taxi owned by the Comfort Fleet:

You are travelling in **COMFORT** with
OWNER: C.H. Tan

Under this was a placard listing the COMFORT PRODUCTIVITY PLAN:

SOCIAL RESPONSIBILITY
Be loyal to Singapore.
Provide camaraderie in COMFORT.
Uphold good image of COMFORT.

SERVICE ATTITUDE
Provide a pleasant journey.
Take pride in service.
Be honest, polite, patient and understanding.
Optimize taxi utilization.

SKILL
Improve skill and knowledge.
Obey traffic regulations.
Maintain vehicles well.

As we edged our way towards the city centre, Mr Tan, a man crowding sixty, asked me if he was adhering to the Comfort Productivity Plan. I assured him that he was a credit to Comfort Taxis and, of course, to Singapore. Mr Tan beamed. He was pleased that I was pleased with his driving skills, with Comfort Taxis, and with Singapore. Visitors must be happy in Singapore, he told me in flawless English. Visitors must feel comfortable here. They must feel they are in a clean, safe place. That is why there were so many rules here. Rules were good for Singapore because rules had made Singapore what it is today. And Singaporeans owed a great deal to their prime minister of the past thirty years, Lee Kuan Yew, for the great changes he had made in their lives.

'He has made us efficient,' Mr Tan said. 'He has made us profitable. He has made us energetic. He has made our living standards the highest in South-East Asia. He has also torn down everything in the city that I remember from my childhood. He has made Singapore unrecognizable. But he has made us profitable. And well-off . . . '

Keeping one hand on the wheel ('Obey traffic regulations'), Mr Tan stuck his left wrist into my face. Strapped to it was a chunky Rolex, the fine print on its face informing me that I was eyeballing a Superlative Chronometer Officially Certified.

'See!' Mr Tan said. 'A Rolex Oyster! Four thousand Singapore dollars new! Only in Singapore could a taxi driver afford a Rolex. This is why we are all grateful to Lee Kuan Yew.'

'For giving you the wherewithal to buy a $4000 Rolex?'

'Yah!' Mr Tan said.

'Don't they sell fake Rolexes on the street here?'

'This is no fake,' Mr Tan said.

'How can you tell?'

Mr Tan committed a major infringement of the Singapore road traffic regulations by momentarily taking both hands off the wheel to strip the watch from his arm. Handing it to me, he said, 'Pull out the pin.'

I did as I was ordered.

'Has the second hand stopped?'

I confirmed that it had.

'See! Real Rolex watch! You can always tell a real Rolex if the second hand stops when the pin is pulled.'

I handed the 'chronometer' back to Mr Tan.

'Nice watch, yah?' Mr Tan asked.

'Nice watch,' I said.

At Orchard Road, I left Mr Tan and his Rolex Oyster Perpetual DateJust and stepped out into a wide-hipped boulevard dedicated to that cultural event called shopping. It was Sunday morning, but Orchard Road was wide awake and hyperventilating. Congealed, but orderly traffic; congealed, but orderly pedestrians. The density of the crowd was bewildering – especially given the time of day, and the day itself. But what was even more befuddling was the way everyone in this disciplined assemblage was armed with brand-name shopping bags: Chanel, Cartier, Armani, Cerutti, Mulberry, Sony, Reebok, Benetton, Ralph Lauren, Crabtree & Evelyn, Levi-Strauss, Adidas . . . Every time one of the traffic wardens gave a decisive 'You move now' toot on her whistle, and a phalanx of Singaporeans swarmed *en masse* across the street, you were presented with a faceless but tidy throng whose separate identities were swamped by the sheer bulk of the crowd. From a distance, the only signs of their individuality were the disparate brand names on the shopping bags they carried.

I watched this scene from behind a screen of mental muslin. Maybe my current state of stupefaction had something to do with the eight hours I'd spent on an aeroplane from Sydney the previous day – a stint of high-altitude incarceration which had left the inside of my skull feeling like a piece of Emmental cheese. Or maybe it was connected with the fact that, on this early April morning, the mercury was reaching for the nineties and the Singapore air had the glutinous texture of half-melted candy floss. Whatever the reason, I found myself rooted to a small patch of pavement on Orchard Road, watching the shopping-bag parade go by, and asking myself: what am I doing here?

I knew the answer to that question, of course. I had come to Singapore to bear witness to a social experiment. Just as I had heard stories about the siren-rigged toilets, so too had I heard that in Singapore you could see a form of communal alchemy at work – a specifically South-East Asian form of communal alchemy, in which the flamboyant virtues of the marketplace had been blended with an anally retentive approach to life. And since the Pacific Rim was now considered to be the *nouveau riche* neighbourhood of global finance, the cheeky new kids on the pecuniary block, it seemed only logical that I dwell for a time in one of its brasher *quartiers*. Singapore, from all accounts, was the most assertive new player in the Asian marketplace – possibly because it was also the smallest of the big Pacific financial centres. A city-state of 3 million simply couldn't match the sheer economic muscle of a Japan Inc. Nor did it possess the venerable mercantile credentials of a Hong Kong, let alone the evolved 'we sell anything' ethos of a Seoul or a Taipei. But, like any ambitious individual, it wasn't content with its secondary status. It wanted – nay, demanded – entry into the fiscal first division. Singapore didn't intend to achieve this objective through guile or Sicilian-style strongarm tactics. Rather, in true Asian fashion, it announced to the world that it would transform itself into a major player on the international financial stage through municipal enterprise and workaholism. It was a society with a game-plan, an agenda – and one which was intrinsically linked to the brave new world of financial services. Viewed from afar, the standard line on Singapore was that it was a fanatically driven, deeply antiseptic nation – Switzerland-on-the-South-China-Sea. Why this need

112

for such diligent industriousness in the pursuit of money? What was it chasing so hard? What made Singapore run?

And, for that matter, why were all these people out shopping in earnest at 11 o'clock on a Sunday morning?

'Keep moving, yah!'

The voice was amplified and tinny, yet it still had a nasty bark. I stirred out of my reverie and looked up into the cone of a megaphone. Behind it was a severe young woman clad in a khaki uniform. Her eyes were shielded by dark glasses, giving her a vaguely sinister Tonton Macoute appearance. The index finger of her free hand was aimed directly at me as she let out another amplified growl:

'*You* – keep moving! No dawdle! Keep moving, yah!'

I suddenly realized why I was the subject of this warden's attentions. I had been dallying on a street corner that was also the junction of a pedestrian crossing. And dallying on the pavements of Singapore was considered a socially irresponsible action – especially if it impeded the steady flow of pedestrian traffic. In Singapore, you couldn't wander aimlessly. You had to keep moving. You had to have a purpose for being out on the streets. You had to know where you wanted to go.

I had no sense of purpose, let alone a destination, so I simply allowed the cascade of shoppers to sweep me across Orchard Road and into a shopping mall called Lucky Plaza. At first sight, Lucky Plaza seemed nothing more than another three-storey concrete box among a crowded thoroughfare of concrete boxes. Only later did I learn that Lucky Plaza was accorded almost landmark status in Singapore, as it had been the country's first modern mall. It was the crude prototype for a programme of architectural transmutation which would irrevocably alter the city's whole appearance. But Lucky Plaza's notoriety wasn't based solely upon its status as a historical site – it was also bound up in its unbridled, free-for-all atmosphere, in being a commercial three-ring circus verging on the hysterical.

You want Ray-Bans, you follow me . . . change money here . . .

I make you suit, two days no problem . . . you want Louis Vuitton luggage, I am the man . . . no one offers you better price for Chinese silk . . . Walkman? Watchman? Discman? . . . new Sony camcorder right here . . . gold necklace for your wife? . . . Chanel bags lowest price in Singapore . . . all compact discs 20 per cent off . . . Sharp laptop computer special offer . . . Panasonic cordless phone special offer . . . Sanyo answerphone special offer . . . Cartier watch special offer . . .

Imagine a choral composition for mixed voices, sung in Chinese-inflected English with lyrics based on hucksterish slogans and performed at *allegro con brio*. Forget Mahler's Symphony of a Thousand. Forget Orff's Carmina Burana or any other raise-the-roof masterpiece. The Voices of Lucky Plaza overpowers them all when it comes to aural force and modern-day spiritual impact. For what is being sung inside this mercantile cathedral is a truly contemporary song of praise. The real New-Age music of our times.

Entering Lucky Plaza was like having your ears boxed. The cacophony was breathtaking. And all around you shops were stacked upon shops, merchants were out-shouting fellow merchants, in the scramble for trade. Compared to this, the souk in Casablanca was as methodical and orderly as a duty-free shop in Zurich Airport. Even in this most disciplined of societies, it was hard not to succumb to the rowdy magnetism of the marketplace.

Ray-Bans . . . Louis Vuitton . . . Walkman . . . Watchman . . . Discman . . . Imitation Rolex copywatch . . .

'What was that about an imitation Rolex?' I asked the short, stubby man in a Filipino shirt who was hissing his offer to anyone who passed by. He immediately put his finger to his lips and nodded for me to follow him. We left Lucky Plaza and walked down Orchard Road to a neighbouring concrete box. As we approached the entrance, the man's eyes nervously scanned the street before he quickly hustled me down a flight of stairs to a plain wooden door. He gave it two distinctive raps with the diamond ring on his little finger.

'Copywatch very illegal in Singapore,' he whispered to me. 'Must be careful.'

The door opened and another short, stubby guy in a Filipino shirt whisked me inside. I found myself in a small whitewashed room, lit by one lonely fluorescent tube. Three trestle tables were clustered together, upon which were laid out rows of fake Rolexes and Cartiers in a medley of models and styles. There were about a dozen other buyers in the room, deep in negotiation with a further quartet of short, stubby salesmen (they must all have been either related or members of a guild for short, stubby copywatch dealers). The noise level in this confined space was again stupendous, thanks to the hard bartering taking place between customers and vendors.

I asked to see an imitation Rolex for my wife, and was introduced to the role of the electronic calculator in Singapore mercantile life. As I came to discover, the bargaining process in this and every other local establishment worked like this: the salesman held a chunky desk-top calculator in one hand, while shouting, 'I make you a price!' He then punched out a series of numbers, which were revealed to you with great ceremony on the calculator's LED display. You immediately shouted out another figure, and the salesman shouted back, 'I make you a better price!' and then proceeded to punch out a new set of numbers on his digital abacus. More shouts back and forth, more numbers punched onto the machine, and after some further dickering, you settled on the sum of thirty-five Singapore dollars (around £12) for an all-but flawless facsimile of a Rolex Oyster – except that the real thing would have run you around two thousand quid.

And when you pulled the pin out, the second hand froze – just like a real Rolex.

The Trade Winds apartment block wasn't really a block – it was actually a set of stacking cubes. Twenty-two cubes to be exact, piled one atop the other. From a distance, it looked like a high-rise Lego set that had been assembled by a three-year-old, as the cubes were stacked at irregular angles, giving the whole edifice a precarious appearance of imbalance. Closer inspection revealed that each cube contained an individual apartment, overlooking a kidney-shaped swimming pool. The Miami Beach Goes Executive school of tropical architecture.

Upstairs, this executive theme was continued, as the door to every cuboid apartment was panelled in the sort of rich mahogany favoured by law offices and corporate board-rooms. Behind one of these doors was Jurgen Kreplin. When he answered my ring on his doorbell, he was cradling a Vodaphone under his chin. Pumping my hand in welcome, he continued his business on the phone, a long stream of idiomatic German pouring out of his mouth as he rattled on about the current state of the dollar. Jurgen was just thirty; an expatriate burgher from Frankfurt, sandy-haired and sinewy. He motioned for me to enter his domain. It was a duplex of stunning dimensions. Vast white walls, parquet floors, twenty-five-foot ceilings, Tizio lamps, low-slung Bau-haus chairs. There was something absurdly archetypal about this scene: an angular, minimalist environment occupied by an angular, minimalist, Vodaphone-connected young-man-of-commerce. It was as if Jurgen Kreplin was doing his best to act the honcho dealer role to perfection. And he *was* a honcho dealer – one of the top commodities traders in Singapore.

'What sort of commodities do you deal in?' I asked after Jurgen got off the phone and ushered me out to a small balcony. At first he ignored the question, as his attention was riveted by two women sunbathing by the pool below us. They were both around eighteen stone and oozed cellulite.

'Shouldn't be allowed,' Jurgen muttered under his breath, then turned his attention back to me. 'You ask me what I deal in? Gold, silver and tin. But I'll tell you what a commodities trader really does. He buys low and sells high. *Verstehen Sie?* – do you understand?'

'*Ja*,' I said.

'Next question, please.'

116

I didn't really have any questions as such. I explained to Jurgen that I wasn't here to interview him; that the only reason I rang him a few days prior to my arrival in Singapore was because we had a mutual friend – a financial journalist in Frankfurt who suggested I look Jurgen up while Out East. Jurgen said that socializing with a friend-of-a-friend was all well and good, but since I was interested in the marketplace in which he operated, and since he had only allocated a 'seventy-five-minute sector' for our conversation, mightn't the time be better served if we restricted our dialogue to the subject of the oil market and Singapore? And, in the further interest of time management, would I now please accompany him to lunch?

Before I could answer, he was leading me out the door, into the lift, and into his Mazda MX-5. He gunned the motor and peeled out of the underground carpark at high speed. As soon as we hit the street, though, he immediately cut out this display of automotive testosterone and obeyed the 30 mph limit. To live in Singapore always meant abiding by the rules. However, to counterbalance the Mazda's measured pace, Jurgen blared heavy metal music: a German band called The Scorpions who were the aural equivalent of a Luftwaffe raid. I stole a fast glance at the pile of cassettes on the Mazda's dashboard: Guns 'n' Roses, Motorhead, Judas Priest, Iron Maiden. A vintage heavy metal collection. I was reminded of something a futures trader had told me in Sydney: dealers always need raucous discord around them in order to function properly.

Jurgen talked blithely on, seemingly oblivious to the electrified din. He talked about his Mazda sports coupé and how it cost him four times as much as it would in Frankfurt, because charging outrageous prices for cars was one way the Singapore authorities kept down the number of vehicles on the road. He told me he'd trained to be a banker and actually did a stint in a Frankfurt and London merchant bank before he discovered the lucrative delights of the commodities market. Then he launched into a soliloquy about the buzz of the trading game and how he'd just closed a silver deal worth $20 million. He also mentioned that he'd eaten Chinese food for the past six nights, so did I mind if we 'went French'?

As was his habit, Jurgen had asked a question to which he'd already supplied the answer, and he steered us into the parking lot of a modern hotel and thence into its French brasserie. A table had already been reserved in his name. The brasserie featured *fin-de-siècle* Parisian décor, piped highlights from *Gigi*, and Chinese waiters in tuxedos. Despite the three-digit temperature outside, Jurgen ordered an avocado pear stuffed with prawns, an *entrecôte bernaise avec pommes frites*, a side order of ratatouille, and a half-bottle of claret. Certain that similar indulgence, combined with my re-emergence into the tropical swelter outside, would acquaint me with a medical syndrome called coronary occlusion, I stuck to a salad and a single bottle of Tiger Beer.

Jurgen inhaled his food, treating it as high-priced fuel that would propel him through the next six hours. Lunch was not a meal; it was a seventy-five-minute sector to be used productively. As there was nothing particularly productive, let alone lucrative, about a chat with a freelance writer, he used the time to talk about himself.

'You know why I left banking to trade commodities? The gamble of it all. And the money, of course. But, *wirklich*, it was the gamble that really hooked me. Plus the pressure of the marketplace. I need pressure to function, to thrive. I mean, you don't have to have the mind of a rocket scientist to trade oil, but you must have the steady nerves and instincts of an assassin. You cannot ever weaken in performance. You always have to be making more. Because you are only worth the value of your last trade. You see, the principle of trading commodities – in fact, of trading anything – is this: you have to make marginally more money than you lose. And at the end of the year, your balance sheet has to show a profit. Result is everything.

'I'll tell you something else – when I compare my skills as a trader a year ago to what they are now, I cannot believe how good I have gotten, how much I have achieved. And it's all due to working in Singapore.'

Singapore, according to Jurgen, was a commodity trader's New Jerusalem. Before coming here, he'd worked for a year in Geneva – but living there was like ingesting a guaranteed cure for insomnia. When his company offered him a transfer to Singapore, he was on the next 747 headed due south-east. Though he knew Singapore couldn't compete with Tokyo as a major-league marketplace, it did have growth potential. Serious growth potential. After all, the Asian market was a boom market. Like an athlete on steroids, it was sprinting past every other competitor in the world financial Olympics. And when it came to trading commodities, Singapore was the Asian city to watch. Especially as it was far cheaper to trade in than Tokyo, where a cup of coffee could cost you ten quid and the annual rent for an executive apartment was about equal to the GNP of Burkina Faso. Singapore was still cheap. It was also fantastically efficient, an infrastructural delight. And unlike Hong Kong, it didn't have a Sino-Marxist gun pointing at its head. Singapore was, in short, *die Stadt Morgen* – the city of tomorrow. For Jurgen, the only real problem with the place was that it was a little obsessed with cleanliness, with rules.

'Singapore is a society where you always have to be con-scious about obeying the law,' Jurgen said, lowering his voice. 'I mean, I sometimes think that the government would pass a law about how and when you could lift your left finger if they thought they could get away with it. Not that I really mind such laws, since everything works here. All right, the place is a dictatorship . . . but it is a visionary dictatorship. As long as you don't criticize the authorities, or interfere with the way society is run here, the Singapore government allows you to make money. A lot of money.'

Singaporeans themselves were really into money, Jurgen said. That was because Singaporeans were, by and large, Chinese – and the Chinese were crazy about lucre. Money to them was the 'Numbah One' factor in life, and they were so fixated with it that they were willing to 'work their asses off' – for this was a nation dedicated to the business of enriching oneself. Singaporeans were proud of their material goods, their standard of living, their success. More than anything else, however, it was money itself – the size of one's bank balance – which was the real measure of financial achievement in Singapore. So it wasn't surprising that many of the older generation of Chinese entrepreneurs didn't enjoy the business of spending money. They might use some of their cash for a decent house, a decent car, but otherwise the idea was to keep it all in the bank and practise extravagant stinginess.

'You can see some of the richest men in Singapore eating at restaurants where a meal costs a couple of bucks. To me, this is craziness. To them, it is caution. And even among the younger generation here, there is still this worry about living well within your means; about saving, saving, saving. And this is why the local girls always want to fuck Caucasians – because their own men only know how to make a buck, nothing else. Caucasians in Singapore also have money, but they also have fun. And if they're not arrogant, they can have their pick of the best girls here. I mean, there are *thousands* of local girls to choose from.

'You know, before I came here, I wondered what the cunt situation would be like. Especially since I'd heard that the single expatriate women in Singapore were usually disasters – which they most certainly are. But the top Singapore girls are the best in the world – though they tend to be a little serious when it comes to trying to get some kind of emotional commitment out of you, especially after you've fucked them a few times. Still, maybe one day soon I will commit to a woman here. I mean, Singapore is a paradise for a married woman. She has all the time in the world to shop, play tennis, have lunch with her friends – because she can turn her housework and children over to an *amah*, who'll look after all that domestic stuff for her. And since all the *amahs* in Singapore are Filipinas, they cost next to nothing. Around two hundred Singapore dollars a month for full-time help. I mean, they're a real bargain. Then again, Filipinas always come cheap.'

Listening to Jurgen talk, I was reminded of an absurd gangster movie I once saw, in which a Cuban refugee, newly arrived in Miami, made the following observation about procuring success in America: 'First you get the money. Then you get the power. Then you get the woman.' In many ways, Jurgen had a similar game plan for Singapore. At the moment he was still trying to get the money aspect sorted out. Jurgen's salary was, by anybody's standards, hefty – around £100,000 a year. To him, however, this was a minimum wage.

'Being rich is not about making six figures. It's not even about making seven figures. It's about liquidity. The sort of liquidity that only an independent entrepreneur can possess.'

An independent entrepreneur. Tied to no company or corporate structure; indentured to no salary. An autonomous magnate, floating high above the executive *hoi polloi*. This was Jurgen's ultimate destination – the financial principality he was determined to occupy well before he reached forty. He had plans. Big plans. Plans that were based around fiscal diversification. When the time was right, he would go solo as a trader and also operate as a big-league consultant to major players in the commodities game. And – 'Since a man also needs an outlet to express the creative side of his personality' – he was already making inroads as an upscale furniture dealer, peddling Deco and Bauhaus paraphernalia to the Asian market.

Commodities and furniture – the foundations of Jurgen's future wealth. And Singapore was the cityscape upon which this structure would be built. It was a logical choice of venue for such a dream, since its facelessness suited such streamlined, intensely focused ambition. As I was beginning to realize, the rigorous sterility of Singapore made it attractive to financiers, for it was a state which had embraced an international hotel lounge aesthetic. There was little to disturb the eye or the equilibrium. That was the peculiar genius of contemporary Singapore – it had been transformed into a distractionless milieu, a realm of pure business.

No wonder Jurgen loved it here. More than anyone else I had met to date, he truly embodied the entrepreneurial ethic. He had tailored himself to fit the role of the myopically ruthless dealer, and acted the part with immense precision, surrounding himself with all its necessary accoutrements (the white-on-white minimalist apartment, the red Mazda MX-5, the Vodaphone, the enlightened attitude towards women). Being in his presence was a curious experience, because he had all but purchased the identity he was now wearing. The corporate honcho image he personified was akin to a suit of protective clothing: when worn, it made him appear invincible; once discarded, you couldn't help but wonder if he would be rendered naked and vulnerable.

Jurgen finished the last dregs of his claret and looked at his watch. Our seventy-five-minute lunch sector was being closed. Jurgen's right hand shot up into the air, two fingers were snapped, a waiter arrived bearing the damages. And I suddenly discovered why Jurgen was so rich so young. When the bill was presented to us, Jurgen pointed to me and said:

'Monsieur will pay.'

And I did. All £60-worth of Singaporean French cuisine.

My place of temporary residence in Singapore was a glass lipstick tube. A twenty-five-storey glass lipstick tube with a hollow interior. When you entered the foyer of this circular structure, your eye was immediately drawn upwards. Above you were tier upon tier of wrap-around balconies, connected to the ground floor by two glass lifts which, when operational, looked like a pair of suppositories in motion.

Living in this high-rise cylinder was like existing in a hermetically sealed suburb. There were restaurants, cafés, bars, swimming pools, and an entire small shopping mall where you could buy anything from electronic surveillance equipment to Chinese silk. A tailor was in residence if you needed a suit made up in less than twenty-four hours. There were a handful of investment specialists on standby to advise you about the intricacies of local red tape, a trio of official money changers and a bureau which could handle all your telecommunications needs. Underground pathways led you to an adjoining supermarket, department store and metro station. The station floors were imitation marble; the trains glistening metal tubes which ran at a whisper. The usual sub-terranean detritus associated with mass transit – cigarette butts, crushed Coke cans, spent condoms, escaped pages of tabloid newspapers – had no place here, as Singapore's lower depths were as antiseptically scrubbed as a hospital operating theatre. There was a good reason for this: the Environment Police – who were also responsible for flushing out non-toilet flushers – were in evidence at every station, just waiting for some poor stooge to enter the underground smoking a cigarette (Fine: £100) or carrying an open can of something fizzy (Fine: £125) or masticating (Fine: £75). Loiterers were also not tolerated, as a Singapore metro ticket is only valid for thirty minutes – a figure calculated on the basis that the maximum length of any journey on the system is twenty-five minutes, so there's no excuse to dally underground for longer than half an hour.

At the end of your metro journey you found yourself traversing another set of underground pathways which led to another office block, another hotel, another apartment block. As I was beginning to discover, life in contemporary Singapore was a linear progression through a series of climate-controlled blocks. It was as if the state's urban planners were doing their best to limit the population's contact with the realities of tropical heat. Cool conditioned air was not simply a source of atmospheric comfort in Singapore. It was a necessary antidote to the year-round soporific dank – a climatic tool which guaranteed efficency in the workplace.

I took the metro to Chinatown. Correction: I took the metro to what was left of Chinatown. This turned out to be a tiny grid of shadowy streets, ill-lit by miserly streetlamps, crowded with old cafés, grubby beer halls, shops trading in dried beef, the occasional food stall. I stopped at one for half a dozen satay sticks and a few Tiger beers. The proprietor – a rotund man in a Ninja Turtles T-shirt – motioned for me to take a seat at an adjoining picnic table. As I ate, he joined me for a beer.

'You like our satay?' he asked.

I nodded yes.

'Cheapest dinner in Singapore. Three dollars, please.'

I forked over the equivalent of one pound sterling. 'That is cheap,' I said.

'Clean, too. The man from the health authority, he visits us three times a week to make certain we adhere to all the sanitary codes. In Singapore, you never escape the rules.'

'Even in Chinatown?'

'Especially in Chinatown. Because we are the only old district of Singapore that hasn't been torn down, they watch us very carefully. The authorities here equate anything old with dirt. Which is why they tore down just about everything old in Singapore. They thought that destroying our past would make us clean.'

I asked the proprietor what the old Singapore was like. He pointed to the sweep of low-lying, elderly buildings with French shutters that fronted the street.

'It was like this. Only dirtier.'

'I shouldn't be talking with you,' she said.

'There's really nothing to fear,' I said.

'It could cost me my career,' she said.

'Don't you think you're being a little melodramatic?'

'That's easy for you to say. You don't understand . . .'

'Understand what?'

'Understand what it's like here. Understand why everybody in Singapore is very taciturn.'

'Okay, so tell me – why is everybody in Singapore very taciturn?'

'It's a protective instinct. Talking about life here can get you into trouble.'

'But I just want to talk to you about your work as a Forex dealer.'

'And, as I told you before, my bank has a policy about their employees talking to the press.'

'I'm not the press.'

'Try convincing them of that.'

'Like I told you – I won't use your real name. Or the name of your bank.'

'I don't really know why you're interested in talking with me anyway. I mean, you're probably like every other outsider who comes to Singapore – you probably think we're all programmed here.'

'You don't strike me as the type who could easily be programmed.'

'Flattery will get you nowhere,' she said with what I detected to be a slight smile. 'Let's order lunch.'

'Do you always eat lunch at eleven in the morning?' I asked.

'You really do ask a lot of questions.'

'Professional habit,' I said.

'A bad habit in Singapore.' Another tentative smile from Isabelle Woo. Smiling, I decided, was something that sent Isabelle Woo into a state of advanced self-consciousness – because, in Singapore, smiling was another civic duty; a way of showing the outside world that everybody was oh-so-happy to be living in such a flourishing, oh-so-efficient society. That was why Isabelle was a bit defensive about breaking into a grin, as it might be interpreted as trying to do the right Singapore thing. Trying to be 'correct'. Or appearing programmed.

Isabelle Woo was self-conscious about a lot of things. She was self-conscious about being a Forex dealer, about eating lunch at 11 a.m. ('I start trading at six, so eleven is a convenient time for lunch'), and about being an unmarried thirty-four-year-old who was still living with her parents.

At first sight, though, Isabelle's appearance belied her omni-present insecurity. Had I passed her on the street, I might have mistaken her for a South American aerobics junkie, as she radiated keep-fit sleekness and Latin chic.

'You wonder why I look like a Latin?' she said. 'My mother's from Caracas, and she met my Singapore father when he was over working in the Venezuelan oil business. Singapore and Venezuela – a curious combination, don't you think?'

Another slight smile from Isabelle Woo as a waiter approached our table and took our order. We were sitting in a small café tucked away in the basement of an obscure shopping centre. At eleven in the morning, it was completely empty. Isabelle Woo was evidently taking no chances about anyone catching us *in flagrante dialogo*. Just as she had taken no chances when, prior to our meeting, she had rung Western Australia and asked our mutual stockbroker friend (who used to work in Singapore and suggested I look her up) if I could be trusted.

'I don't believe in taking chances,' she said. 'Except when it comes to trading Forex, of course. But even there, it took me a long time to learn how to take risks on a position. I really am a cautious person by nature. Then again, I did start out in the banking business as a cashier.'

She never really meant to go into banking. 'When I was growing up here, I had a lot of silly ideas about being an actress – which was not the most practical of notions for someone from Singapore, since we really have no theatre or film industry to speak of. I also had these ideas about travelling the world for a couple of years, but my father, being very conservative, wouldn't hear of it. So, at the age of twenty, I went into the bank. I spent four years as a teller, counting money, doing my sums at the end of the day, and really hating it. Which is why I worked so hard to get a transfer to the Forex department as a trainee dealer – because I knew that was the only way I'd escape from the teller's window.'

She didn't expect to get the transfer to Forex, because

the department was looking for a male trainee. But, in true Singapore style, her initiative was rewarded – mainly because she had kept politely begging the heads of Forex to give her a chance.

'I think they finally chose me because they sensed I was hungry, and also because they liked the idea that I knew nothing about trading Forex, which meant they could train me from zero. When I first joined the department, they explained nothing to me. Just handed me a trading book and told me to start making money for them. I asked my boss how I should start, and he said that the only two words I needed for trading Forex were "bid" and "offer". The problem was, I didn't even know what a bid and an offer were. Of course, they started me off with very small deals so I couldn't lose big amounts of money. But still, the day I made my first loss I was certain that my career was over . . . that I was going to be shipped back to the cashiers' department and never emerge for the rest of my working life.'

I asked, 'Was your first loss that bad?'

'It amounted to less than fifty dollars. But it still scared me. Because I had cost the bank money. Because I had failed. Because I had never lost other people's money before. But, as I discovered, learning how to gamble was part of learning how to be a Forex dealer. My boss made everyone in the trading room play backgammon during our meal breaks because he felt it would help us improve our aptitude when it came to betting. He kept making us bet on things all day – like who was going to walk through the door next, or what the temperature would be at noon, or how long it would take for the coffee maker to brew a pot of coffee.

'But the idea wasn't simply to teach us how to take risks; it was also to get us working as a team. You see, in our dealing room, we can't work as individuals – which is why we have a big sign on the wall that says "Don't Be Greedy!" We have to work as a unit in order to maximize our profit potential. I've seen people fired for trying to play the maverick, for forgetting that they were part of a team, for getting greedy.'

Isabelle said that she worked an eleven-hour day: an exceedingly precise Swiss-movement timetable linked to the opening and closing of other money markets around the world. She was always at her desk by six, when the New Zealand and Sydney exchanges were cranking up for morning business, and she used the first hour of antipodean trading as a kind of mental limbering-up exercise before the big guns in Toyko swung into action at eight. She'd stay with Tokyo until they broke for lunch at eleven, at which point she'd usually make a dash to a nearby health club for a concentrated hour of 'physical maintenance': a fifteen-minute run, a fifteen-minute swim, a fifteen-minute nap by the pool, a fifteen-minute rabbity lunch of salad leaves. Then it was back to the trading room in time for the reopening of the Tokyo market at noon. Four hours later the London market snapped into consciousness, and she tracked its progress until her day ended at six.

Her leisure time was also meticulously planned. Mondays and Thursdays were set aside for filial duties, as she stayed in with her elderly parents. On Tuesdays and Fridays, she took advanced German classes at the local Goethe Institute (German, after English, Chinese and Spanish, would be her fourth language). Wednesdays were always spent taking part in something called 'The Hash' – an international running club which organized a five-mile jog through a different corner of Singapore every week, followed by a boozy barbecue.

And the weekends? 'I belong to a scuba-diving club and a tennis club and a sailing club, so there's always something to do.'

'You obviously enjoy doing things in groups,' I said.

Her smile tightened. 'I do things in groups because I'm not married.'

'No boyfriend?' I asked.

A quick shake of the head.

'No ex-husband or anything like that?'

Another quick shake of the head, and she changed the subject.

'I meet traders from London and New York coming through Singapore who brag about the long hours they work. But to us, an eleven-hour day is quite typical. You see, hard work is an Asian compulsion. In Hong Kong, people work hard to make a profit. In Tokyo, they work hard to impress their bosses. But in Singapore, we work hard to compete in the rat race. Because if you didn't work hard here you'd be seen as different. You wouldn't be ostracized . . . but you would be seen as somebody who simply didn't fit in.'

She leaned forward and all but whispered:

'I shouldn't really be saying this, but a Singaporean's national identity isn't rooted in anything cultural – because we have no culture here. Nor is there much of a sense of national spirit. Have you heard about our "Swing Singapore" days? They take place once a month, when the government deems it necessary for us to go out and have a good time. So they organize some bands and some parties on the streets, and bring out instructors to teach us dance steps. It's systematized fun. Fun without any sense of sponta-neity. Lack of spontaneity is very Singapore. Our national identity is ultimately all about being the fastest-growing financial centre in Asia. And about having a standard of living that is five times better than our parents or grand-parents had.

'What outsiders don't understand is that we're actually proud of our standard of living. I mean, I'm just old enough to remember Singapore before Lee Kuan Yew took over, when ten families would live in one small house. Now there are ten families living in ten houses. That's why we don't mind being organized, why we don't mind all the rules we have to obey, why we don't mind the lack of political opposition – because we all have it so good here. Subsidized housing. National health. No crime. No poverty. No tropical diseases. And plenty of money to spend . . . So tell me, why should we go against the system? Why should we bite the hand that feeds us?'

I had no answers, and simply shrugged.

'Ah, I know what you're thinking! "She's really programmed . . . completely brainwashed."'

Before I could reply, the waiter showed up at our table with two plates.

'Tofu salad?' he said.

The Forex dealer nodded.

The front-page headline of the *Straits Times* – Singapore's one and only newspaper – was a real attention-grabber:

WATER USE BELOW MILLION MARK FOR 2 STRAIGHT DAYS

Water use again fell on Saturday, the second successive day it dropped below the million cubic-metre-a-day mark since the drive to save water started some weeks ago.

But the usage figure was still above the target of below 950,000 cu. a day, which the board hoped to achieve because of the present drought.

This target can be reached if Singaporeans reduce the amount of water they use each day by at least 10%.

Another front-page item from the same day:

SINGAPORE IN THE 21st CENTURY: GIANT SHOW SET FOR JUNE

A multi-million dollar exhibition-cum-show in June will give Singaporeans a taste of life here in the next century.

The show will present a vision of the Singapore of the future, and how Singapore as a global technopolis will offer its stakeholders – comprising citizens and corporations (both local and overseas) – a balanced and attractive living environment.

Serving as a 'visualization' of Singapore in the future the show will indicate how this nation as a cosmopolitan global city can use technology and human creativity to enhance the quality of the life of its people.

Welcome to the cosmopolitan global technopolis, stakeholders. Welcome to the brave new world.

'You probably think we're all programmed here.' Not exactly, Ms Woo. But reading the *Straits Times* was a bit like taking an intensive indoctrination course in the art of keeping your sunny side up. George Babbitt himself would have been considered a downright cynic in Singapore, as his brand of civic boosterism was mild compared to the full frontal 'keep smiling, campers' optimism of the *Straits Times* when it wasn't castigating its readers for forgetting their social responsibility and wasting water. Or engaging in such environmentally dangerous activities as eating sharkskin soup:

SHARKSKIN LOVERS LOATH TO GIVE UP DISH TO SAVE SHARKS
The stomach comes before conservation for many Singaporeans who say they will continue to demand sharkskin soup – even though overfishing is threatening to wipe out the deep sea predator.

Singapore, I was beginning to realize, didn't really have the oppressive flavour of an authoritarian state. It was far too much the enterprising free-marketeer to give in to an atmosphere of totalitarian gloom. The country was more like a rigorous public school, where you wouldn't dare run in the corridors. And, like any strict, elite educational institution, it looked favourably upon students who were pluggers – diligent, hard-working, good at games. But, also like any strict, elite educational institution, it was dubious about original thinking, and wouldn't tolerate pupils who refused to play by the rules.

Playing by the rules was obviously the key to success in

131

Singapore. When I asked Sheila Su Ann why there was this emphasis on collegiate conformity, she replied: 'It's very simple, really. Lee Kuan Yew went to Cambridge.'

Sheila Su Ann had a habit of making comments like that. What made them more disarming was her deadpan delivery and her thoroughly severe countenance. She was a thirty-year-old stockbroker, rumoured to be one of the sharpest young dealers in Singapore. If this city-state was a public school, then Sheila, with her sober suit and sober, assiduous manner, was definitely head-girl material. When I first met her in her spartan office, I expected to spend an hour or so talking with Little Miss Prim. But she followed her remark about Lee Kuan Yew with a shrewd observation about marketplace rivalry: 'Dealing in Forex is all about the getting of glamour; dealing in stocks is all about getting rich.' After that, I began to revise my 'good girl' perceptions of her. Like so many of the traders I was meeting in Singapore, she quickly cast off her veneer of technocratic sobriety once she began to talk about herself.

'You know, one of the good things about working in the Singapore financial markets is that women here are treated with tremendous equality. I spent a week last year in both our New York and Sydney offices, and I was shocked by the attitude of the male traders there – always behaving as if the women traders were their inferiors, as if they had to put up with us. In Singapore, there is none of that. You're judged by your productivity, nothing more. And there are almost as many women as there are men working in the markets here. In fact, around 75 per cent of our graduates in economics or business are women. Because women know that the money as a trader is fantastic, and in a Chinese society money is the only means by which a woman can gain some independence.'

Sheila said that just about everyone she knew in Singapore had gone into the financial marketplace. Those who didn't usually veered off into such pragmatic realms as engineering, medicine, accounting, law, or something on the import/export front. Singapore was not the sort of place where you announced to your friends and family that you were leaping off the corporate carousel in order to get in touch with your alpha waves. Even the advertising game was almost considered a counterculture activity, for this was a society which demanded that its citizenry lead financially fertile existences. If yours was a life dedicated to non-profitable pursuits, you were considered something of a wastrel. And the 'unproductive' found themselves marginalized in Singapore.

'I spent two years in London training as a stockbroker,' Sheila said, 'and I wanted to stay on, but I had a duty to my family to return to Singapore. So I came home, got this job, got married and started a family. I've done all the right things. Everything my family and my country expects of me. And do you know what I've decided? We're all pushovers in this country. We're all trained to do what we're told, no matter what. I'll give you an example: the fertility laws. For a very long time, you were discriminated against if you had more than two kids in Singapore, to the point where only your first two kids could get into the better schools. People stopped having a lot of kids, and the birth rate dipped down so low that the government suddenly got worried about zero population growth. So worried that they now have a new public slogan: "Have Three If You Can Afford It". And people are actually following their advice! We agree to do whatever the government asks us to do. We're so easily swayed. Mr Lee says don't waste water – we go without a shower for two days. Mr Lee says have a third child if you have the money – we go ahead and produce another baby for Singapore. It's crazy.

'And do you know why we always follow orders? Because we've all been brought up to believe that we must please those in authority over us, whether it be our parents or our bosses. We're a society desperate to please – which is why we work so hard. Because we all want to be told how good we are. Because we're all desperate to make the grade.'

★　　　★　　　★

Later that day, I saw an advertisment in the *Straits Times* showing a small child curled up in front of a television in true couch-potato style. Under it was the question:

Is this how your child spends his time during the holidays?

We're not saying you should stop your child from watching television completely. With the pace and competitiveness of life today, a little diversion in front of the television would do your child some good. After all, they are kids and they want to enjoy themselves.

But we would suggest that whatever spare time your child has should be spent productively. And learning to use the computer is, in this day and age, a necessity. Never a luxury.

Then they offered an introductory computer course for four-year-olds.

Thursday afternoon in the lounge of the Singapore Cricket Club. It's an imperial period piece – a dark, high-vaulted room of overstuffed armchairs and ceiling fans and geriatric waiters in starched livery. Outside, the mercury is hitting high blood-pressure levels; in here, the air and the ambience are both refrigerated. The members are men of finance, all dressed in the regulation Singapore business uniform – suit trousers, no jacket, a white shirt with the sleeves rolled down, a nondescript dark tie. Listen in and you'll hear the redundant voices of the Empire – old boys in their seventies who've loitered on in Singapore since independence and still speak with pukka honks and colonial glottal stops. Listen in and you'll also hear the voices of the new technocratic emissaries from the West – the staccato patter of the Dagenham futures-and-options trader; the lugubrious, jowly tones of the vice-president for overseas operations from some lugubrious, jowly corner of middle America; the devious, laid-back cadences of the dealer from the Sydney money markets.

But overriding these Anglo-American-Antipodean inflections is an even more dominant voice – the voice of Chinese-accented English. The voice of Singapore's new burgher class. They have made the confines of this cricket club their rightful stomping ground, for they are its true players now.

Li Su Kong felt out of place here. It was, he said, a salon for the nation's elite, and one which he only used a few times a year because his company had corporate membership. Despite the fact that he was a successful merchant banker, he really didn't consider himself to be a heavyweight financier, let alone a major personage in the Singaporean economic swirl.

'I am just a man trying to earn a living,' he said in a voice that occasionally lurched over a word. In fact, his way of speaking reminded me of a car with faulty suspension: it frequently came unglued when it hit difficult verbal terrain. This gave him a tentative demeanour which was reinforced by his slightly hunched shoulders, his round rimless spectacles, his fact-and-figure-weary eyes. He could have been a cost-accountant, straight out of the John Major school of power dressing. And yet, before he moved into the more tranquil waters of merchant banking, he too was a honcho, playing the money markets as a big-time dealer.

'Why did I get into the markets? A simple matter of money. Ten years ago, after I got my degree, I was working as a middle-management executive in the Port of Singapore, and I was only earning $600 a week. So one of the reasons I took a job in a money broking firm was because my salary doubled immediately – and that was only as a trainee. The other reason was because, ten years ago, money brokers were still something of a rare species out here – even now there are only seven money brokerage houses in all of Singapore. So there was a feeling of being a precious commodity, someone special in the money game.

'After a few years, however, I came to discover that the one and only challenge about being a money broker was making a profit. Once you made a profit, the challenge was simply to make a bigger profit. Of course, making a profit wasn't always easy, and initially I found the pressure very intense. Especially because they were paying me so much more than I ever expected to get paid, and I knew that my survival within the company was based upon continuing to show a profit. So I worried all the time about meeting my targets, about simply surviving as a broker. I worried so much I stopped sleeping.'

Li Su didn't simply suffer from standard-issue insomnia – he actually only lapsed into unconsciousness for around 150 minutes every working night. On the weekends he easily conked out for eight solid hours, but come the working week, his brain would only turn off between the pre-dawn hours of three-thirty and six. To kill time before he reached this mental meltdown, he'd do obsessive things like shine every pair of shoes he and his wife owned. Or he'd drive, cruising in his Nissan through nocturnal Singapore, letting the flow-lanes and one-way systems guide him randomly across the sleeping city. He'd be physically trashed by the time he reached the dealing room later that morning, but a steady intake of caffeine and nicotine would keep him flying at low altitude while he played with numbers. After a while, his body actually adjusted to being awake for twenty-one hours a day – though the price he paid for near-constant consciousness was an eighty-cigarettes-a-day habit and a permanent case of the jitters brought on by the dozen cups of black coffee he imbibed during the working day.

He danced this manic dance on the fiscal high-wire for almost seven years. Inevitably, like all dealers pirouetting on the edge, he reached the point where he realized that he was past his prime; that this was a young person's game and that, having passed the benchmark of his thirtieth birthday, it was time to let some kid take over his desk in the trading room. So he went into banking.

'There are around 140 different banks in Singapore, so when I left the markets I had quite a choice. I decided to work for a small merchant bank, because I thought I might start sleeping a little more if I wasn't with one of the big conglomerates.'

'Are you sleeping better?' I asked.

'Five hours a night now, which for me is a fantastic improvement. But, you know, I think I am one of those people who are destined never to sleep well. Because I am one of those people who always believes he is not doing well enough, who always thinks he should be doing better, who always knows there is room for self-improvement. In this sense, I am a typical Singaporean – never satisfied with myself.'

As it turned out, Li Su wasn't really a product of this workaholic state. He had been born in Shanghai, and was brought to Singapore in 1956, aged six months, when his parents had fled China in search of that age-old emigrant dream – a better life. Singapore had yet to embrace the antiseptic ethos of Lee Kuan Yew, and his parents found themselves living in insalubrious conditions.

'We moved into a village on the outskirts of the city. A terrible place. We had a two-room hut, with no water supply, no electricity, no cooking facilities. We had to get water from a well and cook our food over a fire outside. And my father, who was a taxi driver, was sick much of the time, so my mother had to take on jobs – as a servant and even as a labourer on a building site, carrying bricks to the construction workers. We lived in that village for almost ten years.'

Growing up in such circumstances made Li Su a firm supporter of Lee Kuan Yew – for Mr Lee worked the miracle that he promised Singapore. Under his rule, the septic slums and villages were bulldozed off the landscape. Even the poorest of the populace were housed in adequate accommodation with proper sanitary facilities. All the scourges of underdeveloped tropical life – cholera, malaria, bilharzia, yellow fever, typhoid, polio – were banished. The tap water even became safe to drink. And Li Su and his two younger brothers all made it out of that shanty town and into university.

'Obviously, I have no axe to grind with the government. Obviously, I am pleased with my progress in life – though, as I said before, Singaporeans are never pleased with their lives, because we all live under the shadow of *kiasu* – a fear of failure. Fear and greed are the key facets of life here. Which means that we tend to get over-assertive when we're on a winning streak, and refuse to speak up when we think we're wrong. Mr Lee is a technocrat, and he has transformed us into a nation of technocrats. Frugal technocrats like me who are insecure about money, who worry that it may be taken away from us tomorrow. And because none of us here have big rents or mortgages, we are rarely over-extended like people in the West.'

'What do you do with your money then?'

'I bank it. Or I shop. Shopping is the main leisure activity in Singapore. It's what we do to pass the time. It's how we measure our worth . . . how we gauge just how far we have come.'

Shop ergo sum – was this the true credo of Singapore? Was the notion of shopping as self-validation implicit in the unspoken deal that had been struck between the rulers and the ruled? Without question, a bargain was at the heart of the Singaporean social contract. A Faustian bargain, ice-cold in its logic, which went something like this: in exchange for personal and political propriety, not only will you have the highest standard of living in South-East Asia, you can also buy all the toys you want.

What a shrewd, almost irresistible bargain! Especially since Lee Kuan Yew simply had to point south to Jakarta and Manila, or north to Kuala Lumpur and Bangkok, to hint at the other, more extreme social options on offer in the region. The true ingenuity of his bargain was that it played on the upwardly mobile pride of the Singaporeans, as it contained a seductive subtext: follow my programme of intense self-discipline, and together we will deny our underdeveloped past.

Like so many poor boys made good, Singapore had not only done its best to obliterate all remnants of its mendicant former self; it was also secretly terrified of economic regression. And so it chased its ultimate ambition – to become a world financial centre – with a vigour that was almost spiritual. The pursuit of money here wasn't really about the getting of booty; rather, it was all about the denial of Third Worldliness. There was something almost born-again about the way Singapore embraced the marketplace ethos, seeing financial services and money markets as the means by which to reinvent itself. No wonder the 'enterprise culture' was the true religion of Singapore. No wonder charismatic Christianity was also doing boom business here. Singapore really did see itself as something of a new-fangled puritan, obsessed by the work ethic and determined to fashion itself into a South-East Asian city on a hill – a beacon of mercantile light and clean living in the midst of a pestilential region.

'Many of my banking colleagues have become Christians in the past few years,' Li Su said. 'It's almost a fashionable thing to do – though I think a lot of the reason why there's been such a big evangelical movement in Singapore is because English is now the first language here, which makes it easier for all the big American charismatic groups to proselytize. Also, anytime there's an economic downturn you find more and more people converting. At least five of my friends became born-again after the October '87 Crash.'

'Why weren't you converted at the time?'

'I came out of the Crash relatively unscathed, so I didn't need much in the way of spiritual comfort. Anyway, I'm an atheist like Mr Lee. If I need spiritual comfort, I go shopping.'

Good Friday in Singapore. The financial markets were closed, the shopping malls were open, and in the auditorium of the Ministry of Community Redevelopment, the Evangel Assembly of God was holding a service.

There were three hundred young men and women packed into that rented auditorium – an immaculately well-scrubbed

congregation of young Pentecostalists who (like all Pentecostalists) believed in the power of the Holy Ghost and had
received a 'baptism of the Spirit' which enabled them to talk in
tongues, to heal through the laying on of hands, and to possess
the gift of prophecy.

At first sight, though, this congregation didn't look like
the exponents of shake-rattle-and-roll Christianity one sees in
Assembly of God churches throughout the American South.
They were all far too collegiate and button-down and Chinese
to be Holy Rollers. But when a young local preacher hit the
stage – dressed in the same regulation three-piece Depression-
era suit favoured by roving Bible Belt evangelists – and began
to shout, 'Let's worship Jesus!' this crowd cut loose. All around
me, young Singaporeans started talking in tongues, reaching
for the sky or crying out, 'I thank you, Jesus! I thank you!'

A hymn was sung, in which the congregation let it be
known that they owed everything they were to Jesus. Then
the preacher asked everyone to give Christ a big round of
applause, 'as thanks for what He did for us on the cross of
Calvary'.

And speaking of crosses and Calvary . . . it was Good
Friday, so the preacher wanted to remind us just what Jesus
suffered when He died for us. He gave us a graphic, snuff-
movie account of Christ's treatment at the hands of His Roman
guards. How He was worked over with a cat o'nine tails
'until there was no skin on His back'. How one particularly
sicko officer pushed Jesus's forehead so hard that the son of
God's eyes bulged out. How bone cracked and blood geysered
everywhere when they drove thick rusty spikes through His
hands and feet . . .

'Why did they do this to my Jesus?' the preacher screamed.
'Because the crowd wanted Barabbas to live and Jesus to die.
Barabbas – the sort of criminal we would not allow on the
streets of Singapore, because our wives and children would
not be safe with him around. But the crowd demanded
Barabbas, and Pilate was swayed by the crowd. Just like you

are swayed by the crowd! To smoke. To drink. To take drugs. To womanize . . . Pilate wanted to push his responsibility onto someone else. Just like you blame your parents for what you are today. Or criticize your country for your lot in life, rather than taking responsibility for yourself.

'You must respect your parents, respect your country, and love Jesus. Because your parents never failed you, your country never failed you, and Jesus certainly never failed you. And He never will.'

Responsibility and self-reliance. It was a very Singapore sermon, the perfect homily for a financial city on a hill.

141

SIX

The Forecast Calls for Pain

Laszlo got talking about suicide. He brought the subject up as we sat in a pizzeria near the banks of the Danube, working our way through a couple of large pepperonis with extra cheese. After informing me that this was the first (and, to date, only) pizzeria to open in post-Communist Budapest, he suddenly said:

'You know, I've had a lot of friends who topped themselves in the last year.' As he announced this fact, Laszlo inverted a bottle of East German tomato ketchup and proceeded to decorate the face of his pizza with a big crimson X.

'Lot of despair around these days,' he continued. 'Lot of hopeless vibes.'

'What's the cause of these "hopeless vibes"?' I asked, wondering where he'd managed to pick up the Californian patois.

'Well, if you're living in a country that's going nowhere, you kind of feel despondent. Especially when you begin to realize that you yourself have no options.'

'But surely,' I said, 'upending forty-two years of Communist rule is cause for a little optimism.'

'Yes, it did raise everybody's hopes . . . for around two weeks. But then we all settled back into feeling depressed again.'

I accused Laszlo of hyperbole.

'Accuse me of whatever you like,' he said. 'I simply know this: four friends of mine have made rather dramatic, self-arranged exits from life over the past twelve months. Two from gas, one from pills, one by throwing herself under an express train bound for the Russian border town of Cop. And in all four cases, it was despair about their future which was the trigger.

'Let me explain how this despair works. I have a girlfriend named Illona. Like me, she's twenty-four. Like me, she's a graduate of the economics faculty of the University of Pecs. Like me, she can't find a job that relates to her degree, so she teaches kindergarten, just like I man a spotlight at the opera house. Like me, she earns 10,000 forints a month – that's around £100 in your money. Like me, she lives at home with her parents. And though we talk about getting married, we know it's impossible at the moment because there's a three-year waiting list for an apartment in this city, and it costs several hundred thousand forints in key money if you want to jump the queue. So this depresses us. It also depresses us that we have nowhere to go when we want to be intimate with each other – my parents and I live in a two-room flat that measures exactly 52 square metres, and Illona and her parents and her older sister live in a similar one. We have to borrow a friend's car when we want to make love. It was, I believe, a very common thing in America during the 1950s to make love in the back of a car. Only there they had very big Chevrolets, whereas here Illona and I must make do with a Skoda.

'So, do you see why it's easy to feel a little despondent about one's future here – especially when you have no prospect of a job, an apartment, even a place to lie down with your girlfriend? Do you see why I have serious babe trouble right now?'

Laszlo paused for effect. 'I picked up the expression in Los Angeles.'

Laszlo had just spent six weeks in L.A., visiting an uncle who had fled from Hungary to the City of Angels during the 1956 uprising. The uncle was now a moderately successful Chrysler-Plymouth dealer. He was also widowed and childless, so he flew Laszlo out from Budapest in the hope of convincing his nephew that he had a future as heir apparent to Vavra's Car City in Westwood. Laszlo readily accepted the offer of

a free BUDA/LAX ticket. He didn't say no to the $300 a
week his uncle paid him as a trainee salesman, or to the loan
of an Oldsmobile from the showroom to tool around the
freeways of Southern California. But after six weeks, Laszlo
thanked his uncle for his hospitality and boarded a Tupolev
back home.

'What made you leave?' I asked.

'There is too much sun in California,' Laszlo said.

The sardonic was Laszlo's natural element. He used it as a
defensive weapon, a means by which to insulate himself from
darker thoughts about his current situation. Being sardonic
was, in fact, a national pastime in Hungary, as I'd discovered
on my first journey to Budapest in 1985. I'd arrived late one
March night on a flight from Zurich, and found myself
negotiating immigration formalities in a shed at an airport
that was bathed in a miserly yellow light. The acne-ridden
young customs officers, in drab polyester uniforms with
hammer-and-sickle epaulettes, did their best to put on a
display of surly Warsaw Pact etiquette, subjecting me to an
extended Q&A session about the nature of my visit to the
People's Republic of Hungary and conducting a body search
on a tube of toothpaste in my bag. After being released from
their clutches, I walked out into a small blizzard and spent the
better part of two hours inching my way into the city centre
in the company of a manic depressive taxi driver. He sang an
extended aria about the shortcomings of life under 'Goulash
Socialism' – Communism with a token private sector, the
brainchild of the then Hungarian Socialist Party leader, János
Kádár. As the driver discoursed on such subjects as the need
for Party membership in order to get an adequate flat, the
headlights of his Lada cut through the cascading snow to
pick up the red stars and slogan-packed billboards ('Together
We Will Build the Socialist Future') which lined the road in
from the airport. In the midst of his monologue, a bulletin
came over the car radio, announcing the death in Moscow of
General Secretary Constantin Chernenko. Without missing a

beat, the cabbie said: 'You know why Chernenko wore such big shirts? . . . Because he had a Soviet pacemaker.'

It was my first encounter with Hungarian mordancy. Now, five years later, Laszlo re-introduced me to this trenchant brand of *Mitteleuropa* melancholia. We met on the metro in central Budapest. It was a dank June afternoon and I'd just arrived in town, having taken the bus in from the airport to the city centre. That ride into Budapest Centrum had been something of a revelation. Gone were the red stars and the propaganda hoardings which had once lined the airport road. In their place were billboards for Samsung, KLM and Lotto. Satellite dishes decorated the suburban skyline of a capital which had once jammed foreign broadcasts. Near the airport was a curious sight – a small log cabin with an American flag stretched across its side. Ten yards away was an old Socialist Realist statue of a Noble Youth, his left foot permanently frozen in a resolute 'Onward, comrades' pose. Seen from afar, it looked as if this Young Pioneer was marching purposefully towards kitsch Americana.

These cosmetic signs of transformation suggested that I had arrived in a nation undergoing an ideological *volte face*. Eight months prior to my arrival, the old post-war Communist order gave in to popular will (not to mention the dictates of *perestroika*) and cleared the way for the first free elections in over four decades. The Party was swept from power, despite the fact that Party members had rapidly ditched the *ancien régime* of János Kádár and run for office as reform-minded socialists. But before their collapse as a political force, they had done something seriously revisionist for a Communist government – they had set in motion plans for the creation of the first Hungarian stock exchange since the coup which brought the Party to power in 1948.

And this week, the exchange was opening for business.

Having just spent time in an Asian society which had embraced the free marketplace with near-religious fervour, I was curious to see a social landscape which had suffered a complete loss of faith in one economic system, and was now gambling its future on the competitive magic of mammon. I had a hunch that to visit Hungary now, in the interregnum between the death of state socialism and the premature stirrings of *laissez-faire*dom – would be to enter a society whose entire perspective on the uses of money was under review.

But it wasn't just attitudes about lucre which were being re-examined here; so was the name of almost every street and metro station in Budapest, as I discovered when I climbed down from the airport bus to a metro station called 'November 7 Square', but which also had the name 'Ocktagon' officially printed below this. I turned to the man standing next to me on the platform and asked what was the real name of the station.

He turned round. He wore a *California Über Alles* T-shirt and Wrangler jeans, coupled with a smile that revealed faulty dental work.

'There are two answers to your question. For those still stupid enough to be dedicated members of the Party, this station is called November 7 Square, because that was the date of the 1948 Revolution. For everyone else in Budapest, this station is now known by its pre-1948 name, Ocktagon.'

'But what's it called officially?' I asked.

'Officially it is called November 7 Square and Ocktagon. However, in two years' time, it will only be called Ocktagon. You see, everyone wants to get rid of all the street and metro names that the Communists imposed on the city, but everyone also realizes that to change all the names back to what they were before 1948 would cause widespread confusion. So, for the moment, we are a capital with two names for half our streets and metro stations. It is a Hungarian solution to a Hungarian problem.'

As we rode the metro through the crumbling tunnels of the underground system, Laszlo Tompa told me about himself. He was an economist by training, but had been reduced to operating a spotlight at the opera house, as there was little work in the Hungarian financial sector at the moment. There was a première of a new ballet at the opera house this evening, and he'd sneak me in if I was interested.

'It's a big night for me,' he said. 'I'm the man who gets to keep the spotlight on Jesus Christ.'

That evening, after ditching my bags at a hotel, I showed up at the opera house and settled down in a spare seat at the back of the stalls to watch the first performance of something called *Mamma Maria*, a full-length ballet concerning the life and times of Christ, danced to the recorded music of Bach. It was a curious entertainment. Scenic Holy Land backdrops which looked like the Biblical paintings in a Jehovah's Witness brochure. A barefoot Jesus *en pointe* as he gave the Sermon on the Mount. Lazarus breaking into a two-step jig after being raised from the dead. Mary Magdalene showing off a lot of leg. A trio of dancing centurions tossing Christ around the stage as if he were a beachball. Jesus vanishing up to heaven courtesy of a pair of suspension wires. Mamma Maria (a.k.a. Mary) lifting up the cross and tossing it over her shoulder into the orchestra pit. And, finally, a vociferous chorus of disapproval from the audience as the curtain fell.

'I don't think we have a hit on our hands,' Laszlo said as we met up after the performance.

'I've never heard booing like that,' I said.

'Do you blame them? Finally there is the freedom in this country to speak openly about Christianity, and what do we get? Dancing centurions and Jesus on twinkletoes.'

We hopped into a taxi and cruised down Nepkoztarsasag, the main thoroughfare of Pest (the flat western sector of the city, in contrast to Buda – the hummocky eastern flank), which was surely destined for a new name, as *Nepkoztarsasag* is Hungarian for 'People's Republic'. It was an avenue of baroque imperial design which, back in 1985, had struck me as a little haggard and shopsoiled from years of neglect. Of course, Eastern European capitals are often cast in a monochromatic tinge of ramshackle despair. But tonight this boulevard of pockmarked black stone suddenly regained a semblance of old Hapsburgian grandeur. The ballet had ended early, and Budapest was swaddled in an amber, malt whisky twilight. As the taxi crossed the Danube, the castellated clifftops of the Buda hills defined the horizon. Looking downriver at the sequence of rococo bridges joining Buda to Pest, the gold dome of the parliament building catching the last vestiges of dusk, it was easy to convince yourself that this was a golden, magisterial capital of abundant possibilities.

When we reached the pizzeria, and Laszlo started bragging about the country's suicide rate ('We even exceed Finland on a *per capita* basis'), I couldn't help but wonder if it didn't have something to do with Budapest's ability to throw off its dour countenance and radiate an aura of heartbreaking promise. To see the city glow with such deceptive optimism, and then to consider the hopeless limitations of your own situation, might just prove too unbearable . . . and might just push you over the precipice.

Laszlo kept topping up his pizza with ketchup, the crimson X's diminishing in size as he worked his way through it.

'Have you seen this film *Wall Street*, by Oliver Stone?' he suddenly asked.

I nodded.

'I liked this film very much,' he said. 'I especially liked the milieu it depicted – the milieu of the golden boys.'

'But they were depicted as a bunch of assholes,' I said.

'Precisely,' Laszlo said. 'The moral of the film was a very simple one: if you are going to work in the financial markets, you must be an asshole. To me, this was a very intelligent point of view. I mean, if I was to get a job on the new stock exchange here, I would work very hard at being an asshole. It would be my principal goal in life.'

'Have you tried to get a job on the exchange here?'

'Of course I have tried, but the stock market is still very new and very small, so the opportunities are limited. But it is my goal; to be a big-time Hungarian stockbroker and an asshole. It is an honourable ambition, no?'

'I'm sure you'll go far,' I said.

'For the moment, I am going nowhere but the opera house. And I might not even be there for much longer, because we are talking about having an all-out strike.'

The threatened strike was about a wage hike that the staff and artists were demanding from the Ministry for Culture, but which the government refused to approve. After four decades of 100 per cent state subsidy which allowed the management to keep ticket prices down to an 'opera for all' price of around £2 for the best seat in the stalls, the ministry was now making rumblings about the arts in Hungary having partially to pay their own way. Budapest was a serious theatre town. On any night of the week there were about sixty-five different productions on show, and every playhouse (from the state opera company right down to some backstreet fifty-seat studio space) was wholly dependent on the largesse of the government. But now, as a marketplace ethos inveigled its way into all corners of Hungarian life, there was talk of grants being slashed; of theatre companies being forced to look to the private sector for funding; of the survival of the commercially fittest.

'Everyone wants a market economy,' Laszlo said, 'but nobody wants the end of state funding for the arts. It is a very confusing time.'

Laszlo's father was finding life in post-Communist Hungary particularly confusing. He was a labourer in his late fifties, and had once been a member of the Party.

'He joined the Party after the uprising of 1956 because he felt it was the only political force that could give the country the stability it needed. And he remained faithful to the Party for more than thirty years. But, you know, he's never been more than 200 miles from Budapest; he's never wanted to see the world. So Communism suited him because it kept him insulated. And even though he's now working for a German tool manufacturer, and probably earning more money than he's ever earned in his life, he's still very uneasy about this thing called democracy. It actually frightens him, because it's riddled with uncertainties. My mother is the same way. She's a cleaner in a laboratory, and she still believes in Communism simply because it offers absolute predictability: here is your job, here is your allotted living space, here is your subsidized food, your subsidized health care, your subsidized holiday. To them, the free market is the unknown. And they are terrified of the unknown.'

'Just like you?'

'Just like everybody in this country.'

We left the pizzeria and crossed the Danube back into Pest. Laszlo stopped and pointed to a grubby concrete office block, shuttered and derelict.

'We used to call that place the White House,' he said.

'Why?'

'Because it was Communist Party headquarters. Now it's empty. The new government keeps trying to rent it out, but nobody wants it. Nobody wants to work there. It's a dinosaur. There's now talk of tearing it down and putting a little park on the site. I think that is a very good idea. It is a piece of history we can live without.'

As Laszlo spoke, a BMW came careening around the corner at 70 mph, forcing us to jump back as it grazed the pavement.

'Asshole,' I yelled after the glossy black German machine.

'Lucky asshole,' Laszlo yelled even louder.

In the urban geography of the Warsaw Pact, Vaci Street held a special place. It was a landmark, a showpiece – the only shopping precinct within the socialist countries that was a reasonable facsimile of a high street in the West. A visit to GUM in Moscow or the Markthalle in East Berlin (prior to reunification) introduced you to the ascetic realities of *Ost Bloc* consumerism. They were nothing more than a ragged assortment of merchants hawking cheap bits of glass, vinyl jackets, jars of pickled gherkins, and second-hand false teeth.

Compared to their impoverished church-bazaar atmospheres, Vaci Street was pure glitz. Here, in the mid-1980s, you could see the quasi-materialistic face of Goulash Socialism – small state-run delicatessens brimming with foodstuffs; old-style haberdashers and dressmakers; a handful of well-stocked bookshops; and a department store that sold low-grade replicas of Japanese electronic durables. There was even a small Pierre Cardin outlet. And though the vast majority of Budapest's citizenry couldn't afford its prices, they still bragged about the presence of Emporium Cardin on Vaci Street – as if the arrival of a Parisian designer on their own, more parochial version of the rue Saint-Honoré conferred on them a certain cachet; an illusion that they weren't completely cut off from the spoils of the West.

Now, however, there was no longer any need for such illusions, as the West really had arrived on Vaci Street – with a gaudy vengeance. Gone were the spartan window displays, the elderly awnings covering nondescript shopfronts, and the state advertising hoardings with upbeat slogans like 'Buy Shoes in a Shoe Shop'. In their place had come the marble façade of the new Estée Lauder shop; the neon of McDonald's; the bright, primary, monocultural colours of Benetton and Stefanel; the aerobically sleek window displays of Adidas. Gone too were the little men selling *Nepszabasdsag*, the Hungarian *Pravda*. They'd been replaced by newspaper vendors hawking the *Herald-Tribune*, the *Frankfurter Allgemeine Zeitung* and *Bild*. Outside Estée Lauder, locals watched with bemusement as a trio of hard-bodied models demonstrated a new brand of lip-gloss to the syncopated accompaniment of disco funk.

To walk down Vaci Street at eleven on a Monday morning was to enter a Bartholomew Fair of nascent capitalism. The cafés were packed. Briefcase-carrying men and women were marching purposefully in and out of the new office blocks and international trade centres which lined the precinct. Elderly peasant women were taking advantage of this open market-place to work their way through the crowd, selling pieces of embroidered linen and cheap handicrafts. There was even a lengthy queue waiting to gain admittance to the Adidas establishment.

To the new arrival, the buzz of Vaci Street was tangible, a buzz which announced that the new-look Budapest was wide open for business. But this buzz was deceptive. Though the street was black with people, and though you had to cool your heels for thirty minutes before inching your way into Adidas, little in the way of true commerce was taking place anywhere else, since Western prices were being charged for the booty on offer. As Laszlo had told me, the average wage here was around 10,000 forints a month (£100), so how could anyone justify a Stefanel shirt for 3040 forints? Or a 4000-forint Walkman at the new Sony outlet (though a McDonald's *Tejurmixok* – a milkshake – was manageable at 60 forints). Only visitors from the West actually bought anything in these new emporia. The only reason there were such phenomenal crowds at Adidas was that a pair of designer trainers had become the foremost symbol of street-cred in democratic Hungary. People saved for months to afford a pair.

Vaci Street was, in effect, an open-air shopping arcade, where plate glass functioned as a sort of borderline, a reminder that even if the reinforced boundary between Hungary and the West had tumbled, a formidable frontier still existed between material aspirations and individual economic realities. In the past, Hungarians looked on enviously from afar at the spoils of the West. Now the spoils were within their physical grasp on their capital's main street . . . but all they could do was still look on with envy.

At the top of Vaci Street was a shop with a bank of television sets in its window, which repeatedly broadcast a Paul Simon video. Crowds would gather in front of this window and sing along as he asked:

> Who'll be my role model
> Now that my role model is gone, gone . . .

On Vaci Street in post-Communist Budapest, this was a pertinent question.

It was a relic from an ostentatious age, from a time when financiers had a penchant for the gaudy, the monumental. It was an antique, once declared bourgeois and decadent. Not since Wall Street had I seen a house of commerce so steeped in extravagant art deco: ornate statues, marbled floors, stained-glass chandeliers, cathedral-like ceilings. It could have been the Babylon set from *Intolerance*, the mansion occupied by Citizen Kane. Actually, it was the Budapest Bank.

There were ladders everywhere, supporting painters who were attempting to restore some lustre to the walls and mouldings after four decades of official neglect. And there were doors everywhere; corridor upon corridor of doors. I climbed two flights of stairs and ran into a pair of elderly functionaries engrossed in a game of draughts. I mentioned a door number; they pointed to another corridor. More doors, more numbers, then another flight of stairs, then yet another corridor. Just as I was beginning to wonder if Franz Kafka had been a Hungarian, I reached door number 5302 and found Istvan Kiss behind it.

'Very impressive,' Istvan Kiss said, looking at his watch. 'You are exactly two minutes late. You must have an excellent sense of direction, because most of the time I find visitors roaming the halls, begging anyone for information as to the whereabouts of my office. Twenty minutes is the record so far for a guest to be adrift.'

He suddenly put a finger down the back of his shirt collar and began to scratch vigorously. It was a thick white collar, soaked in sweat. Large patches of perspiration had also formed around his underarms, and droplets of moisture clung to the edges of his Zapata-style moustache.

'Excuse me, please,' he said, his index finger now exploring the nether regions of his neck. 'The heat in this building is terrible. We've yet to learn about air conditioning in this country.'

As he talked, two women burst into his office, greeted him, and marched through a rear door. Like Istvan, they were both in their thirties, and showing visible signs of fatigue.

A moment later, another man flew into the office, interrupted our conversation by handing Istvan a sheaf of documents, then flew out through the other door.

'A busy office,' I said.

'A crazy office,' Istvan said. 'Especially with the stock exchange opening this week. But it was worse last year when this office was set up to reinvent the entire Hungarian stock market from nothing. Since none of us really knew what we were doing at first, things were absolutely insane.'

Istvan Kiss was a member of the Securities Exchange Committee. It had been set up in 1987, when Hungary began a process of gradual economic liberalization, and twenty-five Hungarian banks and financial institutions signed an agreement to coordinate the trade of securities. Five years earlier, the Hungarian government had begun a gradual movement towards a market economy when it passed a law sanctioning the issuing of bonds – a profoundly radical move for a Comecon country during the Andropov years. But Hungary had always been making quasi-radical moves on the economic front since 1968, when János Kádár – the First Secretary of the Hungarian Communist Party – eliminated orthodox Stalinist planning as part of his programme of Goulash Socialism. In its place he implemented a whole new financial system using Western-style budgets. But it was still incredibly difficult for, say, a municipal council to obtain any sort of credit from the National Bank of Hungary to finance local projects. So, in 1983, after fourteen years of deliberation ('An extraordinarily short amount of time by Communist standards,' Istvan assured me), the Kádár regime gave the go-ahead for the creation of a very limited securities market – a market in which only state-owned companies or local councils could issue bonds which would underwrite worthy communal projects (along the lines of that new sewerage system your town had its heart set on).

Now, as every ambitious local bureaucrat in the country quickly discovered, a bond issue was an impressively fast way of raising money to get things built. As the number of bond issues increased during the eighties, and as the bonds themselves grew in value, it became obvious that a mercantile arena in which they could be traded was needed. Once again, however, the Ministry of Finance hit the 'caution' button and didn't broach the idea of a proper stock market until 1987, when Gorbachev was firmly in power in Moscow and the Hungarian Politburo felt confident enough to introduce a two-tiered banking system (which, in turn, gave birth to two dozen or so credit banks). Only then did the ministry dare to raise the ante further by proposing the creation of the first securities exchange in the Eastern Bloc. In the winter of 1988, the first 'stock exchange days' since 1948 took place once a month in an office in central Budapest. Within a year, the market was meeting once a week. By early 1990, the new traders of Budapest were gathering together every Tuesday, Wednesday and Thursday. And now, beginning this week, the Hungarian stock exchange would be a daily event.

'In the best of all possible worlds,' Istvan Kiss told me, 'we would have located the new stock exchange on its original site. But since that's now a studio in the state television company, we had to abandon that plan – unless we wanted the market to look like a game show. So, what we decided to do was take a big public room on the ground floor of this bank and rebuild it as a new exchange. But since that's going to take at least another year, we've rented a room in the International Trade Centre on Vaci Street, and set up a makeshift stock market there. It's not exactly the most spacious of trading floors, but after forty-two years of waiting, we can all cope with a little claustrophobia.'

Istvan happily admitted that he'd only learned the difference between a stock and a bond in the last four months. He was a mathematician by training, and had dabbled in computer programming after graduating in 1977. But he threw up the software game and did something vaguely irrational: he became a tour guide.

'To someone from the West, it must sound crazy to leave the computer business for a job taking groups of Hungarians to Munich and London. But when I found out from my brother-in-law in the State Travel Office that I could make five times as much money as a tour guide, plus get free travel out of the country every other week, at a time when most citizens were only allowed a trip to the West every two years, I immediately took the job.

'You see, this was the craziness of the old system – the fact that educational qualifications meant nothing. In fact, the more degrees you had, the less money you probably earned. So, for eight years I was very happy with my twice-monthly trips to Germany or Britain, not to mention the hard currency I saved out of the expenses they gave me in Deutchmarks or pounds.

'But after my thirtieth birthday, the idea of leading groups of my compatriots through Westminster Abbey and the Hofbrau House for the rest of my working life began to pale. So I was faced with a dilemma: what should I do next? I decided that, with Hungary starting to move towards a free market, the finance business was the future here. I went back to university, took an advanced degree in foreign trade, and ended up here. In other words, I got lucky.'

A mathematician turned computer boffin turned tour guide turned deputy head of the Hungarian Securities Exchange. Istvan had stumbled into high finance to escape a future without prospects on a state sector salary. Judging by the procession of young financiers streaming through his office, the stock market in Budapest was in the hands of a bunch of post-graduates. You could almost sense their bemusement at finding themselves in charge of an actual financial exchange – and in their own country to boot.

'Most of us on the Securities Exchange Committee still

haven't an idea of what we're doing. I was worried about my lack of knowledge until I got talking last week to a visiting bond dealer from New York. When I told him I still didn't know the first thing about running a market, he said: "That makes you perfect Wall Street material."

'Do you think he was serious?'

Outside the Budapest Bank, I met a very different breed of Hungarian financier. He was bearded, and fat in a sausage-and-beer sort of way. He wore a grubby pair of jeans and a grubby windbreaker. As he approached me, he whispered the two words which are the *lingua franca* of all Eastern Bloc hustlers:

'Change money?'

I asked him the going rate for twenty pounds sterling. He said 3000 forints – around 50 per cent more than I would have got in a bank. I did a quick scan of the street. Seeing no uniformed cops in the vicinity, I said, 'All right, let's do it.'

He motioned me into a small passageway between two buildings. I watched him pull out a wad of forints and count out fifteen 20-forint notes. As he offered me the money, I felt a hand grab my shoulder. A badge was flashed in front of my face. Before I knew it, the moneychanger had shoved the forints into the breast pocket of my jacket while simultaneously snatching the £20 from my hand. Hissing 'Move quickly . . . don't turn back,' he was gone with the wind.

My adrenalin shot into overdrive. Black marketeering was a serious offence in Hungary. Keeping my eyes focused firmly in front of me (and remembering the time-honoured rule of villainy: never run away from the scene of a crime), I walked as calmly as possible down the passageway, never once turning around, but expecting the strong arm of the law to land on my shoulder again at any moment. When I reached the next street, I cut down another passageway, losing myself in the crowd queuing for lunch at McDonald's. At the counter I ordered a chocolate *Tejurmixok*, and pulled out the wad of forints still scrunched in my breast pocket. A 20-forint note covered the wad. But instead of fourteen other 20-forint notes, I discovered eight 5-forint notes wrapped in it.

I stared at the bills, flummoxed. A switch had been made. The guy with the badge had been working with the black marketeer. I'd been stung. And stung brilliantly.

'Sixty forints, please,' said the fast-food clerk. I handed him my pile of notes. Twenty quid for a McDonald's chocolate milkshake. Capitalism was alive and well in Budapest.

Three days later, while having a beer with Laszlo, I told him about the short-con job that had been perpetrated on me. He immediately pulled out a copy of a local newspaper and pointed to the front-page headline: Head of Budapest Black Market Found Murdered.

'What were you doing last night?' he asked.

The International Trade Centre on Vaci Street was a curious hybrid. It was a new building, kitted out in the raiments of global corporate culture – pseudo-marble walls, tubular lighting, duty-free arcades, hotel-style conference rooms, a telecommunications centre, an in-house bank, computer monitors with up-to-the-minute prices on the Frankfurt, Paris and London bourses, and the ambient sound of Muzak.

An instrumental version of Elton John's 'I Guess That's Why They Call it the Blues' was playing as a dozen or so people entered a tiny conference hall on the first floor. The hall had a sign on its door: *Targyalo* – Negotiating Room. Inside was a small semicircle of modern, German-designed wood and steel desks, each equipped with a Hyundai computer and a phone. In the centre of the room was a moderator's table with a microphone. Overhanging this was a state-of-the-art electronic board to keep score of the proceedings ahead.

You could have fitted the entire new Hungarian stock market into the sitting room of my South London flat. It was a pint-sized bourse, a newborn decked out in expensive baby clothes.

The dealers were virtual newborns as well when it came to the business of stockbroking. With the exception of one elderly man, all the traders were around twenty-seven years old. Looking at them settling down to their computers, talking amongst themselves, working the phones, I had to remind myself that they were the first generation of Hungarians to have entered this mercantile arena in over forty years. In fact, they were the practitioners of a business that had been proscribed until very recently. And, as Dieter Momper told me, they were probably the only stockbrokers in the world to hold degrees from Karl Marx University.

Dieter Momper was a young dealer from Frankfurt, 'Our Man in Budapest' for a major German brokerage consortium.

'My company knows there is little profit to be made here for three or four years. But they also know that this is a market which will undoubtedly expand. Especially since, given the freedom, Hungarians have an innate ability to make money. So we believe this is a bourse with a big future. Which is why we decided to get a toehold here from the outset and – how shall I put it? – get a piece of the action.'

Dieter wasn't the only foreigner sniffing around the new Hungarian stock market. Behind the semicircle of trading desks was an informal cluster of American, Japanese and British versions of him. The first bourse in the post-barbed-wire Eastern Europe had become something of a tourist attraction for international financiers on the 'joint economic venture' circuit.

A young woman took a seat at the moderator's desk, turned on the mike and (according to Dieter, who became my unofficial Hungarian translator) essentially asked the dozen assembled brokers, 'All right . . . who wants to trade some stocks?'

The exchange was open for the day. But, with only thirteen stocks listed, the market didn't exactly crackle with wheeler-dealer energy. Like the Casablanca bourse, the trading atmosphere here was low-key, almost subdued – though the steady stream of souk-like chat indulged in by the Casablancan dealers had little place inside this *targyalo*. Once trading began, gossip stopped, and Hungary's stockbrokers concentrated completely on the business at hand. Their diligent, almost studious involvement with every transaction underscored their newness at this game. It was oddly touching, their intensity of purpose. They were like learner drivers – excited about being behind the wheel, but fanatically over-cautious. They weren't going to take their eyes off the road for a moment.

When the moderator asked if anyone felt like getting the exchange day rolling, there was a deafening silence for about five minutes, occasionally interrupted by a telephone conversation between a dealer and a client. Finally, someone bought 200,000 forints'-worth of shares in Hungary's only department-store chain, scoop, at a price of 186 per cent – a transaction which amounted to a little under £3750. A few minutes later, 300,000 forints in bank bonds were purchased at a share price of 76 per cent – a deal worth about £2300.

'Hey, this is truly amazing,' one American observer said as he watched a transaction register on the electronic board. 'We got a guy here who's actually bidding against himself.'

'That's one way of keeping things moving,' a colleague said.

The remaining thirty-four minutes of trading yielded a grand total of ten transactions. In its first week of official life, the Hungarian stock exchange was still learning to crawl.

'The money involved here is still negligible,' Dieter said as the dealers began to close down operations for lunch. 'I mean, I've seen deals here for as little as £150. Still, it is early days. And every stock exchange once started like this – a few people standing around a little room, trading with each other. Only here, at least, they're using software, which gives them an idea of what trading in a big grown-up exchange is like.'

Bela Jansco was perhaps the only dealer there who'd had

first-hand experience of what it meant to operate on a full-scale trading floor. At the age of seventy, he was the oldest stockbroker now trading on the new Budapest stock exchange. Forty-two years ago, however, he had the distinction of being both the youngest and the last stockbroker to trade on the old exchange. When the Budapest stock market was declared ideologically null and void in 1948, Bela Jansco was like a footballer who'd been shown a permanent red card and told that he'd never be able to compete again in the game he lived for and played so well.

'Stocks have always been my great professional passion,' Mr Jansco told me after Dieter had introduced us outside the *targyalo*. 'So to be back here, in a financial marketplace, in the company of other brokers, and actually trading securities again . . . well, for me, it's almost like being reunited with a long-lost love and being told that you can build a life together again.'

At first sight, Bela Jansco totally contradicted the identikit image most of us have of a venerable stockbroker. No pin-striped suit. No speckled braces. No paunch reflecting years of carvery-and-claret lunches. Rather, he was a ruddy, powerfully built man with hardened hands and a formidable grip. Had I not just seen him on a trading floor, I might have mistaken him for a farmer, decked out in the one antiquated suit he owned, who'd come up to the big city for the day. Until a few months ago, this first impression would have been correct – before the exchange reopened, he'd been running a small chicken farm on the outskirts of Budapest. After we sat down for coffee in the Trade Centre's café, he told me that chickens were just one of many pursuits he had been engaged in during the forty-two years he'd been forbidden to deal in securities.

'Back in '48,' Jansco said, 'not only was I the youngest trader in the market, I was also a partner in my own brokerage firm: Szabo and Jansco. When the Communists closed down the exchange, it was a disaster for me and every other stockbroker in Budapest. Still, at first it didn't stop us from dealing. For the next four years a bunch of us kept the Budapest stock market alive by holding private trading sessions in darkened rooms around the city. In a sense, it was a very exciting period – let's face it, it's rather unusual to be part of a clandestine stock market. But it was also terribly dangerous, since that was the era of Stalinism, and if you were caught engaged in any sort of free-market business, the penalties were frightening.'

Eventually the secret police became aware that a floating stock exchange was alive and flourishing in backstreet Budapest, and Jansco and his fellow traders had to abandon their covert activities. Desperately in need of work, Jansco fell back on his ability to repair cars, and landed himself a job as a technician in the Hungarian Automotive Traffic Institute.

That job lasted until the 1956 uprising. Jansco played an active role in that event, thereby rendering himself *persona non grata* with the new regime which the Soviets put in place after they terminated the insurrection with extreme prejudice. Not only did Jansco lose his job at the Traffic Institute, he found himself blacklisted from any other proper employment. Many other former brokers voted with their feet and fled the country, but Jansco's family commitments compelled him to stay.

So Bela Jansco – one-time golden boy of the Budapest Stock Exchange – spent several years supporting his young family and elderly parents by picking up occasional labouring jobs. He cleaned houses. He hauled coal. He worked on building sites. He also set aside two hours a day to read through any economic journals or foreign newspapers he could lay his hands on, to keep abreast of what was happening in world finance.

'I may have been hauling coal, but I was still aware of how the market was doing in Vienna, Frankfurt, Paris, London . . . This became an obsession of mine – to follow the market, to remain intellectually involved with it even if I couldn't actively participate in trading.'

Six long years passed before Jansco was finally allowed to seek normal employment. He found a dreary job as a purification inspector for the state water board. It was a job he was to hold for twenty years, until 1982, when he reached retirement age. 'That was the year the government started to liberalize the economy a little bit,' Jansco said, 'which made me decide it was time I set up my own economy. So I moved out of Budapest altogether and started a small private farm where I raised poultry. But though I was now in the chicken business, I still followed the market. And I remained up to date with all the new computer technology being used in trading. You see, I was convinced that, given the gradual movement in Hungary towards a mixed economy, the day would come when a stock exchange would be operating in Budapest again.'

In March 1988 an international conference was held in Budapest to help generate foreign interest in the future resurrection of the Hungarian stock exchange. The conference organizers advertised in the press, saying they wanted to track down any old dealers from the pre-1948 days, and Bela Jansco knew he was on the way back to the brokerage business. He put on his thirty-year-old suit, cleaned the mud off his farmyard shoes, dug out the brittle documents from the 1940s that proved he was once a member of the Budapest stock exchange, and caught the train to the capital. At the conference he was introduced to Dieter Momper's bosses from Frankfurt, who were looking for a venerable local broker to work with their young representative in Budapest. Not only was Bela probably the only extant dealer from that era, but he also demonstrated a phenomenal grasp of the new electronic world of international bourse-dom. They grabbed him immediately.

'What do I think of computers on the stock exchange?' he said. 'I think they are wonderful. In the old exchange, we had to write prices by hand. Computers make the flow of information much faster, so I am happy to use one – though I must say this: trading principles in 1948 and trading principles now are basically the same.'

'Aren't you bitter at all?' I asked, amazed that throughout our conversation Jansco never once expressed rancour about that forty-two-year enforced absence from his beloved world of stocks.

'Bitterness is a useless emotion,' he replied.

'But you were a successful broker with your own company, and they took it away from you. How can you not be resentful?'

Bela Jansco gave me an untroubled, 'that's in the past' shrug. 'All I feel is immensely sad that so few stockbrokers from 1948 are still alive to see the Budapest exchange back in operation.'

'But how did you keep yourself going during all those years of terrible hardship?'

Jansco smiled at me: 'I put my faith in God, and in the classic economic theories of Adam Smith. And my faith has been rewarded.

'By the way,' he said, rising from his chair, 'if you're thinking of buying shares in any of our new public companies, tourism and transport are a safe bet.'

Then the oldest new stockbroker in Budapest excused himself and returned to the floor of the exchange.

Iren Kovacs wore sadness as if it were an eau de cologne. Her eyes were picture windows of melancholy; she found the act of smiling physically daunting. She was anorexically thin, a petite, auburn-haired woman in her late twenties, stylishly dressed in black lycra. And yet, her aura of unhappiness was engaging. It brought out that dumb male urge towards protectiveness. You wanted to put your arms around her and say something Bogartesque like, 'Forget it, sweetheart, it's only Budapest.'

I met Iren in a bar with an unfortunate name: The Fraggot. It was a dark, wood-clad pub down a backstreet of decaying apartment blocks. Laszlo dragged me there on one of our frequent nights on the razzle.

'I come here to meet girls,' he said as we settled down at a table.

164

'I thought you were engaged,' I said.

'I come here to be an asshole,' he said.

Iren and a friend were sitting opposite us. Laszlo became transfixed by Iren, turning to me and shouting over the clamour of voices and jukebox music:

'I am in love with this woman.'

'You work fast,' I said.

'I always fall in love with women who have problems. And this woman has big problems – I can tell.'

'You are American?' the woman with big problems suddenly asked me. I nodded, and Laszlo blanched with embarrassment as he realized that she spoke perfect English, and must have understood everything he'd said.

'I have lived in America with my husband and children,' she said.

'You have kids?' I asked.

'Two,' she said. 'A girl six, a boy one.' Laszlo turned a little whiter.

Iren introduced herself and her friend Vera, a bubbly chucklehead who punctuated her conversation with frequent bursts of the giggles. Laszlo instantly turned his attention to her, leaving me to ask Iren where she had lived in the States.

'You know Gainesville in Florida? My husband Zoltan was at the university there, doing a doctorate in theoretical physics. Three years in the Florida sun – it was nice. But we had next to no money in America, and I was pregnant with our second child, and Zoltan was worried that our little daughter was becoming too Americanized, and then he was offered a position back here in the main scientific institute, so . . . '

She attempted a smile, and failed. The transition back to the limitations of Hungarian life had been a trial, she said. The only apartment they could find was one large room – around 60 square metres – with a tiny alcove where the children slept. She and her husband made do with a mattress in a corner next to the galley kitchen. And though Zoltan was a highly respected young physicist, he was only making the usual Hungarian starvation wage of 10,000 forints a month. She had found a job in a small firm of stockbrokers, which paid even less: a mere 8000 forints a month. At least the work was interesting, as the whole idea of being employed by a brokerage house was still such a strange and wondrous notion in Budapest. And she was hoping that this private sector job might give her some professional scope for the future.

'I am just working with the stockbrokers now as an assistant,' she said. 'But I think this might be a way into bonds. I want to be a trader – and for one simple reason: I want to make proper money. At the moment, the struggle here is terrible. We have the wages of an Albanian and the taxes of a Swede.'

She tried another smile, but again she couldn't quite pull it off.

'You should come by our office sometime,' she said. 'Meet my boss, Josef Bonnay. An unusual man for Budapest. Twenty-nine years old. Very ambitious. Very rich. Very much an acquired taste.'

So, a few days later, I dropped by the offices of Bonnay and Schiff. They occupied the first floor of an old administrative building near the Danube – a grandiose Hapsburgian relic, built around the sort of cobbled courtyard that looked as if it had once been used as a training ground for Lippizaner horses. Scaffolding shrouded the building – a commonplace sight in contemporary Budapest, as more and more former state properties underwent private gentrification, courtesy of companies like Bonnay and Schiff.

The suite of rooms that housed this stockbroking firm had been given the no-cost-spared treatment. Iren met me at reception, and led me through a conference room decked out with imitation Louis XIV furniture and a massive table worthy of strategic arms negotiations. A towering pair of mahogany doors led to the inner sanctum of Josef Bonnay – an office the size of a small public park, with a limousine-length desk occupying centre stage. As I quickly found out, Josef Bonnay was one of those people who would have gone mad in a small confined room. He needed a wide-open space to accommodate his corpulent 6'3" frame and his habit of being unable to sit in a chair for more than thirty seconds at a clip. He was constantly going walkabout in his office, cordless phone in hand, talking in machine-gun bursts.

'Coffee? You want coffee?' he asked as he pumped my hand. 'My coffee is the best in Budapest. Iren, please, two with milk . . . Now, you want to know about our company? Okay, sit here in this chair and I'll tell you everything you want to know . . . but I must also tell you that I am running the office single-handedly because my partner is in Frankfurt, and I myself am driving to Vienna in twenty minutes' time, so I will have to talk fast, okay?'

I sank into an overstuffed armchair, like a spectator at a private entertainment, and watched Josef Bonnay perform. It was quite a show as he roamed every centimetre of his office while engaging in a rapid-fire monologue that was punctuated by frequent telephone interruptions, the arrival of Iren with 'the best coffee in Budapest', and a quick dash into the en-suite bathroom for a fast gargle with mouthwash when his vocal chords began to resist the pressure he was putting them under.

'Every boy has a dream,' he began in pseudo-documentary, 'cue heartfelt music' style. 'Mine was to become a stockbroker. Growing up in a socialist country, I knew this dream would be considered impossible. But I saw movies about stockbrokers, read books about stockbrokers, and I developed a very simple ambition: I would be a stockbroker. And I would be rich.

'Now, when I received my economics degree from the University of Pecs in 1982, the government was just beginning to experiment with economic liberalization by authorizing the first bond issue in Hungary. So I joined the National Bank of Hungary, because I knew that this bond thing had possibilities, and the only way to change the system was to work within it. A year after my arrival, I made my move – by convincing my bosses that they should open the bank's first National Bond

Office and let me run it. Initially, they were incredibly sceptical
– I was only twenty-three at the time and earning 3500 forints
a month, a ridiculously small sum, about £35. But I eventually
talked the Deputy Governor of the bank into giving me a shot.
He told me: "All right, I'll give you $800,000 in hard currency
to set up a bond trading division, but if you lose the bank's
money, I can assure you that you will never do financial work
in Hungary again."

'Of course, in the first five months of running the bond
division, I tripled the bank's capital. But I was still only earning
3500 forints a month. I realized I would have to set up my
own company. But what you must understand is that, in
1984, *perestroika* was an unknown word, and though we had a
small private sector, the economy was completely centralized.
So the idea of even thinking about being a stockbroker –
let alone setting up your own brokerage business – wasn't
simply revolutionary: it was still a little dangerous. Especially
for someone like me who'd never joined the Party.

'So I had to wait until 1987, when there was another big
period of economic liberalization, before I could leave the
bank and team up with an old university friend to create
Bonnay and Schiff. And in just over three years, we've almost
become rich. Do I hear you ask how? It's simple, really: we put
in fifteen-hour days and managed to issue just over one-third of
all bonds in Hungary. And the issuing fees have been fantastic.
I mean, in our first year of business, we increased our capital
from 65 million forints to 250 million forints, and last year we
had an 85 million forint profit after tax.

'Now, I know what your next question will be: how has this
success changed me? Quite honestly, I do not feel changed. All
right, I have bought this suite of offices for 2 million forints,
and I drive a BMW 531i, and I own a 1.5 million forint
apartment in the Buda hills, and I was able to take my wife
and two children on a holiday to Disneyworld last month . . .
but really, it hasn't changed me. Because, you see, I always
believed I was destined for this sort of financial success. And

also because my partner and I both feel we are having our faith in Hungary rewarded. In 1984, many of our university friends from the economics faculty headed west to Austria and Germany, but we weren't tempted, even though we were told there would never be a Hungarian stock market during our lifetime. But it is here. And in five years we have been able to achieve real financial wealth in our own country. We think Hungarian. We feel Hungarian. We are Hungarian. So what's wrong with being rich Hungarians at the same time?

'At the moment, however, everyone is very suspicious of our success as a company. Hungary is, at heart, a very suspicious nation. When people see you driving a BMW, they immediately assume that you've been cheating someone or doing dirty deals. I mean, we've been investigated twice by the Ministry of Finance simply because we've done so well. Of course, they have found no wrongdoing because we are very honest in this office. Unlike the former regime. You know what happened when I was at Disneyworld? I ran into an old *apparatchik* from the Finance Ministry – a real hardliner – coming out of Mickey's Castle. Incredible! I mean, how could he afford a trip to Mickey's Castle on a state pension? Where did he get the hard currency? I'll tell you where he got the money – he siphoned it off the top for twenty years. Opened up a discreet dollar account in Zurich or Geneva. Of course, he turned absolutely red when he saw me. But then he tried to be friendly, tagging along when we went on a ride on the monorail, buying my kids hotdogs. It was unbelievable – this old bastard of a Stalinist eating a hotdog next to Snow White's House. You know what I finally said to him? I said, "The Party is obviously rewarding you well for years of service." And the son of a bitch replied: "*Perestroika* is a wonderful thing, Josef."

'So you see the legacy of the past that we're up against? For forty years, Hungarians were force-fed the idea that capitalists were evil incarnate – and at the same time, they knew that the Party was a pack of thieves. How can you blame people for being distrustful of anyone with money? We are going to need five years minimum before there is no longer this suspicion of money and financial success, before we gain the people's trust. This is why the stock exchange is so important – because, through share issues, we can create an investor society. What this country needs urgently is a middle class.'

I finally opened my mouth: 'And what role do you see for yourself in this new middle-class Hungary?'

'I will be its John D. Rockefeller, of course.'

He looked at his watch.

'I can give you three more minutes. Perhaps you would like me to pose for an official photograph?'

Josef 'Rockefeller' Bonnay was disappointed to learn that I didn't have a camera with me.

Iren was right: Josef Bonnay was an acquired taste. He was, in many ways, a big kid – and one who'd come of age at just the right moment. Had this been the Hungary of ten years ago, he would have either spent his life languishing as a bureaucrat in the State Bank, or he would have headed west over the border. But timing is everything in life, and Josef had lucked into coming of age in the era of *glasnost*, and had caught a ride on the Hungarian Free Market express. No wonder he was simultaneously cocky and vulnerable. He knew he was poised to become one of the first big financial success stories in democratic Hungary. And it was patently obvious that he saw himself as an empire builder who was determined to establish outposts of Bonnay and Schiff in London, Frankfurt, Paris, Tokyo, New York and, of course, Vienna. He had even worked out an interview-*shtick* for visiting writers and journos, in which he portrayed himself as an Eastern European go-getter bound for glory – the boy from the socialist world who probably read *What They Don't Teach You at Harvard Business School* in *samizdat* and dreamed big capitalist dreams.

'*Perhaps you would like me to pose for an official photograph?*' Already Josef was preparing himself for the inevitable 'art of the deal' autobiography that some desperate Budapest hack would be hired to ghost in a few years' time. And yet, I found it easy to tolerate his vaingloriousness, especially since it masked such obvious insecurity. He had created a role for himself as a Budapest version of the Wall Street whiz, and he was desperate to play it right – especially in the presence of a Westerner. But as he had been raised in a relatively doctrinaire Communist society, and his knowledge of Wall Street was limited to print and celluloid images, he had to improvise like crazy. It was rather endearing, his frantic attempt to exude club-class confidence. He reminded me of an immigrant who had landed in a new world and was determined to assert himself by going straight to the top. Only, in his case, that new world was a region of his own country, a place still beyond the ken of the majority of his compatriots. He really was a frontiersman in Injun Territory – a fully-fledged man of capital staking out a claim for himself in an economy still bound up in the meagre security of state socialism.

'Survive?' Iren asked me as I left Josef's office.

'He's not the worst,' I said.

'Everyone I know hates him,' she said. 'My husband Zoltan especially – he thinks Josef's completely overbearing and pushy. I tell him that pushiness is what's needed in this country at the moment. But Zoltan never listens to me. Or anybody.'

Another fruitless attempt at a smile.

'I am in a dark mood today,' she said. 'We had Laszlo and my friend Vera over for dinner last night. It was a catastrophe.'

'Laszlo and Vera? He really does work fast.'

'Very fast. Right after you left the pub the other evening, he disappeared with her. My one night out in three weeks and I end up on my own.'

'What happened at dinner?'

'Not much, really. Zoltan and Laszlo took an instant dislike to each other and got into a terrible argument about politics.

Then Vera drank too much and started crying about missing her two children.'

'Vera has two kids? But I thought she was only twenty-three.'

'She is. And she had the two kids with two different fathers, both of whom were separately granted custody of the children.'

'No wonder Laszlo went for her. He did say he prefers women with problems.'

'I want to go back to Florida,' Iren said. 'People have fewer problems there.'

'That's not my experience of Florida.'

'Okay, people have the same problems, but they have more money.'

'But won't you eventually have more money here?'

'Perhaps,' Iren said. 'But even if we do, we will still work very hard at being depressed.'

Tibor Konrad was a man with a problem. A semantic problem.

'I will explain my problem to you. I am the publicity officer of the Socialist Party – which everyone believes is still *the* Party, but which we have been telling them is simply *a* party, nothing more. So the source of our public image problem comes down to the difference between the definite and indefinite article.'

I asked Tibor if this grammatical confusion was the reason the Socialist Party had received only 10 per cent of the vote in the recent general election.

'Eleven per cent,' he said. 'A very creditable result too, considering that the election was all about changing the entire political system of the country. And it is an especially good result when you remember that everyone was expecting the complete annihilation of the Party.'

'But you said you weren't *the* Party?'

'This is true. We broke with the orthodox Communists years ago – when Kádár was ousted in 1988 and Karoly Grotz

172

became the new General Secretary. So, politically, we have no association with Kádár's old Hungarian Socialist Party. However, our party chairman was a former Foreign Minister and a high-ranking member of the old Party – so I guess you could say that our party is filled with one-time members of *the* Party who wanted change, which is why they joined the Socialist Party – since we fully supported Hungary's move towards democracy.'

Listening to Tibor, I was reminded of an old Marx Brothers routine about drawing up a contract, in which much ado was made of the fact that 'The party of the first part is equal to the party of the second part . . . ' I was also reminded that, amidst all the born-again free marketeers, there was still a small but distinctive segment of the Hungarian population which continued to embrace the tenets of socialism. Tibor Konrad was, by virtue of his position, their spokesman – an urbane and articulate former diplomat with a weakness for Marlboro cigarettes and Ralph Lauren clothes (his V-neck jumper, his shirt and his denims all displayed the familiar polo insignia), positioned behind a cheaply veneered desk in an office that was the epitome of low-wattage, dingy civil servicedom.

'I was First Secretary at our embassy in Canberra when the Party essentially abdicated last year. So, as a member, I was naturally called home. Whereupon I immediately joined this new party. Because, though I felt the old Party was a thing of the past, I still believed in social democracy. And since the new Socialist Party was ultimately social democratic, it seemed the obvious party for me.'

I began to understand why Tibor had a semantic problem. The word 'party' had dominated his life from an early age. During the war, his parents had been sent to Auschwitz for the crime of being Jewish. The Soviets liberated them, and after the Communist takeover in 1948 his father became a senior journalist on the leading Party newspaper.

'The Party was an integral part of my childhood. I went to Party schools, Party summer camps, and became a member after university. Of course, I always knew that it wasn't a democratic organization. Just as I always knew that Hungary was simply the happiest barrack in the Soviet camp. But I honestly believed in socialism as the doctrine of the future – especially since the Party in Hungary broke with proletarian internationalism and placed a far greater emphasis on social issues. And I still believe in socialism today. The reason the old Party had to die was because, much as Kádár tried to cast off his past, he was still tainted by the ghost of Stalinism. But, you know, this "yoke" thing, this idea about Hungary being trampled underfoot by the Kremlin, is completely overblown.'

I mentioned the words 'nineteen fifty-six'. Tibor agreed that the nation had been temporarily trampled on – but the achievements of Mr Kádár in the following years made up for 'all that unfortunate repressive business'. Why then was Mr Kádár so unceremoniously ousted from power in 1988? His time had passed, Tibor said, reminding me that, as a certain V.I. Lenin once noted, socialism is an evolutionary process. So evolutionary, in fact, that the sort of moderate Marxist-Leninism espoused by Mr Kádár had now been superseded by the social democracy espoused by Tibor and his Socialist Party.

'As a party, we agree in principle with the idea of privatization. However, our concern is how we privatize our industries, and whether we stand by while our economic sovereignty as a nation falls into foreign hands. Of course, we want to see an end to centralization, but this insane headlong rush into the free market is going to cause much misery. Everyone talks about *laissez-faire* economics as if it were the new religion, the answer to all our ills. The fact is, though, that the vast majority of the people here can barely afford what's in the shops at the moment – so you can imagine how they will feel when privatization robs them of their job security; when they are asked to pay for health care; when their rents are trebled by private landlords.

'I tell you this – we may be out of favour now, but in two years' time we will be considered the true party of opposition in this country. Because what we will be offering the people is most of the social benefits they enjoyed under the old regime, with none of the repression. This new crowd in power are only interested in money, in getting rich.'

I remarked that at least under the new government in Hungary the ability to live comfortably no longer depended on whether or not you were a member of the Party. This observation did not go down well with Tibor Konrad.

'Don't believe all the lies being told by the Budapest *nouveaux riches*. The vast majority of the people in power now are well educated, widely travelled, live in the best places in the capital, and drive Western cars. And none of them, to the best of my knowledge, were ever imprisoned by us.'

'But the Party *did* imprison those who opposed it.'

'Very, very rarely. This was not Romania, for God's sake. Anyway, look at the old Party *apparatchiks* now. They all live in prefabricated houses and drive Ladas at best.'

'Wasn't a Lada considered as much of a status symbol when you were in power as a BMW is now?'

'Perhaps . . . but at least no one drove anything fancier than a Lada or a Skoda back then. And, you see, one of the reasons I am confident about our future as a party is the knowledge that the proletariat will not like the sight of fat cats in BMWs on their streets – especially when they themselves are struggling to survive.'

'I thought you said that your party had broken with the whole idea of "the proletariat"?'

'No socialist party *ever* breaks with the proletariat,' Tibor Konrad said.

Laszlo leaned against the bar of The Fraggot and contemplated the inside of his beer glass.

'Today I went for a job interview,' he said. 'An American firm of accountants. They're opening an office in Budapest, and are looking for Hungarians who can use a calculator. They asked me why I wanted to be an accountant. I think they wanted me to tell them that I had always dreamed of being an accountant, that accounting was the noblest profession on earth. But all I could say was: "I will take any job that gives me proper money."

'That was obviously not the right answer. One American on the interview panel said: "Is money all you're interested in?" I was very stupid, and I told him: "Everyone in Hungary wants as much money as they can grab now. Because money – real money – is the only way out of the collective mediocrity of the last forty years. I want proper money so I can have a proper life."

'A proper life is not much to ask for, is it?'

Someone behind the bar slipped a cassette into the stereo, and we listened silently to a Chicago blues number, 'The Forecast Calls for Pain':

> Coffee for my breakfast,
> Shot of whiskey on the side.
> The forecast calls for pain.
> My baby's comin' home,
> And the forecast calls for pain.

The singer wailed on, predicting bad times ahead. And Laszlo turned to me and said: 'This man is definitely Hungarian.'

SEVEN

The New Jerusalem

Stan Gould opened the door of his studio flat and said, 'Welcome to my palace.' The flat was a small rectangular box in a new development on the Thames near Wapping. It did not have a river view. Instead it looked out over a gaping wound in the East London landscape – the half-dug foundation of another luxury apartment complex that some developer had abandoned after his business went belly-up. This hole in the ground had become a rubbish tip; so too had Stan's flat. Though it was, ostensibly, a contemporary apartment – with a modern fitted kitchen, recessed lighting and a video-intercom security system – Stan had filled it with junk-shop furniture, borrowed from charitable friends and relations. There was a broken-down sofa-bed covered in green imitation leather, an aluminium kitchen table with a red formica top, an outlandish chunk of Axminster carpet, a fifteen-year-old colour television, and a three-foot stack of newspapers which functioned as an end-table.

There were newspapers scattered on the floor as well, along with half a dozen or so mugs. The mugs were filled with spent teabags and drowned cigarettes. Two half-empty bags of sugar sat on the kitchen table next to a bottle of milk which was beginning to resemble a penicillin culture. In the midst of this testament to Good Housekeeping stood a forty-three-year-old man in an Armani suit which was in need of urgent dry cleaning. He smiled, but I couldn't help noticing that his eyes were like billboards advertising *Weltschmerz*. We were passing acquaintances, friends of friends who'd hooked up for the occasional boys' night out over the past few years. We'd fallen out of touch, and it was only when I ran into another mutual friend at a party that I learned about Stan's changed circumstances and decided I owed him a phone call. He seemed surprised to hear from me – and even more surprised that I'd managed to track down his new phone number – yet he immediately invited me over to his new abode.

'Very stylish, don't you think?' he said, motioning for me to perch on the one corner of the sofa-bed that wasn't covered with smudged cigarette ash. 'I've really moved up in the world.'

'Like the suit,' I said. 'You working?'

'Job interview.'

'Any joy?'

'No one's hiring middle-aged, out-of-work FOX dealers these days.'

'How can you afford the flat then?'

'Got a small consultancy thing going with an old client of mine. Covers the child support payments and the rent on this kip. But it doesn't stretch to new furniture, as you can see.'

'You seem to be bearing up nonetheless.'

'Guess so, under the circumstances. But I'm still waking up around dawn, still jumpy as hell, still thinking that today's the day I'm going to fuck up royal down at the exchange – even though I haven't been near the floor in months. I'll tell you one good thing, though – at least when I wake up I don't think about the desert anymore.'

'The desert?'

'Yeah, the desert. That was all part of it. That was a sign of things to come.'

From 1988 to 1990, Stan would snap into consciousness at five o'clock every weekday morning and think of the desert. And in the screening room of his mind, he'd unspool a film in which he was cruising down a long, thin strip of tarmacadam that bisected a flat, empty quarter of sand. He was somewhere in North Africa, riding tall into the geographic equivalent of infinity on a venerable Triumph chopper, and dressed in the raiments of an 'action man' – broken-down leather jacket, faded denims, aviator shades, a white silk scarf lassoed around his neck. The curious thing about this scene was that it had no plot to it. He wasn't being chased by a platoon of Libyan commandos; he wasn't shooting down that narrow smudge of blacktop to rescue some svelte Scandinavian archaeologist who'd fallen into the clutches of Bedouin from the wrong side of the desert. There was no plot to this mental film-loop; only that image of himself thundering through that ceaseless void, the gritty desert air hitting him full-frontal in the face as he made a kick-ass beeline to nowhere.

But then the film would suddenly break, the screen would be flooded with light, and Stan would be transported back to his bedroom in Little Venice and his 5 a.m. grogginess; a grogginess that was quickly replaced by the 5 a.m. globule of acid which hit his stomach every morning as his body gave him a pointed reminder of the amount of Scotch he'd thrown back the night before as he steeled himself for another day speculating in commodities.

Stan was a commodities trader on the London FOX – the Futures and Options Exchange. Check that: Stan was a commodities dude. A honcho. A player. And one of the top dealers in town, clearing around 300k before bonuses. What's more, though many of his contemporaries had already burned out by their forties – or had been deep-sixed by their companies – he'd managed to stay in the fast lane. His profitability had been consistently Olympian, and he saw himself as a shrewd politician who knew how to negotiate that malevolent labyrinth called corporate life.

Stan had always considered himself deeply street-wise. And for one simple reason: he saw himself as a street kid made good. 'I'm a Thatcherite classic,' he told me when we first met. His was an archetypal story of the entrepreneurial eighties: the kid from Stepney, his father a bus conductor and his mother a hospital cleaner, who'd started out at eighteen as a runner on the floor of the stock exchange and had managed to stay on the escalator marked 'Up'. The past decade had been good to him. In 1980, he'd made it to the position of trainee on the trading desk, pulling down a respectably suburban 12.5k. Eight years later he was the company's senior broker, and his salary had done a twenty-five-fold leap into the top tax-bracket stratosphere.

What was the secret of his success? Supreme shrewdness when it came to playing the numbers game of commodities trading, no doubt. And also a lucky break when his company was absorbed by a major American multinational in 1981. His new M.D., a 'Colorado guy' named Jack Jasper, immediately took a shine to the kid from Stepney because (as he later told him), 'You're not like the rest of the public school assholes we got here. You know what's it's like to hustle, to claw your way up. Which means you're my kind of Brit.'

What Jasper didn't realize was that Stan secretly envied just the kind of Brit he himself despised. He envied their poise, their disgusting self-assurance, their 'born to rule' aura. He envied their Oxbridge degrees (Stan had hit an educational dead-end after O-Levels), and their OBE'd fathers who, with a phone call or two, procured them entry to the commodities game at a level which it had taken him twelve years to reach. Most of all, he envied their clubbiness – their sense of exclusivity; of belonging to an elite principality within a common realm. Even though Stan knew that these *noblesse oblige* chaps respected him for his financial wizardry, he always got a strong whiff of their loftiness whenever he dealt with one of them. He knew that, to them, he'd always be the kid from Stepney, the bus conductor's son.

Angela always told him to ignore these residents of Twitdom – they might talk posh, but none of them was pulling down 300k like him, so why should he worry if they looked down their thoroughbred noses at him? A bloke's salary was what counted these days, not his accent.

Angela was often giving Stan little gems of professional

advice. Whenever he mentioned a small crisis at the office, or his growing fears that his career as a top commodities hustler would soon incinerate, his wife would spit out some platitude, a verbal Band-Aid to staunch the flow of his anxiety. When he complained that the whole commodities game was riddled with a particularly ruthless breed of cowboy, she replied: 'Live in a jungle and you're bound to meet some animals.'

Angela had turned into a walking needlepoint motto. She also traded in such well-known conjugal banalities as 'We hardly talk and we never touch no more.' It was as if their marriage had been reduced to the lyrics of some cheap country-and-western lament; as if they were inhabiting a cliché of their own making. Most mornings – as he dragged himself to the loo, self-consciously squeezing the promontory of fat which overhung his pyjama bottom – he found himself wondering what wrong set of directions had landed the two of them in this cul-de-sac of tired phrases and dreary bromides.

Maybe it was the money. After all, when they first met they survived quite happily on Stan's middle-management wages and Angela's on/off earnings as a temp, living in a one-bedroom flat near Clapham Common. But now he was pulling in this huge, operatic salary, and they had all this . . . stuff.

Stuff – that's how Stan referred to their worldly possessions. The new £340,000 house. The new Volvo 480SE (not to mention his company Jag). The Venezuelan au pair for their seven-year-old son Jason and their five-year-old daughter Jennifer. The furniture by David Linley. His suits from Paul Smith and Armani, her dresses from Jasper Conran. The holiday in St Lucia. The riding lessons for the kids. The personal aerobics trainer for Angela . . . It was all . . . stuff.

And the thing about such accoutrements was, once you had them – once you eventually broke down and gave your AMEX gold card a coronary by buying that chunky Rolex at the Zurich Airport duty-free – you kind of felt . . . vacant. And almost disillusioned by the discovery that finally having the watch you'd coveted didn't really change anything; didn't make you feel any more high-powered or hyper-monied or the possessor of bigger *cojones*. At least, that's how Stan always privately felt after buying some major luxury item or consumer durable.

But, hang on . . . this wasn't the way a 300k commodities dude was supposed to be thinking, Stan told himself while lathering his face in preparation for an assault by his cut-throat razor (Sheffield steel and a pure ivory handle, £60 at Trumpers. Why do I buy such toys?). If you were putting up with ulcer-inducing twelve-hour days – not to mention the constant company of some of the most conniving sharks in London – the least you could do was get some pleasure out of all the lucre coming your way.

But the thrill was gone. The thrill was dead.

Not for Angela, though, he told himself. Angela still got a charge out of all that hard-bartered-for jack. And she knew how to spend it. So much so that they were servicing a £20,000 overdraft. 'I make 300k and I'm still in hock 20k to the fucking bank. And why? Because Angela's always buying something. Born to shop, that woman. Trying to buy her way out of coming from Romford. Thrice-weekly sunbed treatments and a £20 facial every Friday. She won't let me touch her for months, then she tells me I'*m* being distant, I'm not interested in her, I'm all wrapped up in cocoa, sugar, coffee. And she's definitely doing the dirty behind my back with some other bloke.'

Maybe it was the way she'd momentarily turn away when he asked her what she'd done with her day. Maybe it was a certain hardness he could glimpse in her eyes, which all but telegraphed the message, 'I need you for the money, but nothing else.' Maybe it was the *cordon sanitaire* she'd erected in their bed. Whatever it was, he knew. And he felt helpless in the face of it all. Just as he felt helpless in the face of her demands for more dialogue, more interaction. Inter-what?

★   ★   ★

Open outcry was the type of trading Stan engaged in on the London Future and Options Exchange. A bunch of dealers stood around a ring and screamed their larynxes out in one concentrated burst of hysterical barter. It was a very basic, old-fashioned brand of capitalistic gambling with millions of pounds as the table stakes – a very adult, potentially calamitous game which began every workday morning at nine.

Around that time each day, Angela would steal a glance at the kitchen clock and conjure up an image of Stan, in shirtsleeves, standing smack dab in the middle of the FOX ring, caterwauling his head off as he bought and sold sugar futures. After a couple of hours he'd dash out of the exchange and into the nearest pub for a double Glenfiddich – 'the morning steadier', he called it, the first of five or six 'steadiers' Stan would imbibe during the course of the day. For Stan was an alcoholic, although he refused to acknowledge the fact that he was running on 90 per cent proof.

Open outcry – Angela always liked the sound of that expression. She envied Stan the ability to howl in the name of commerce, and simultaneously divest himself of all that pent-up anger, all that internal sound and fury. She'd love to engage in a bit of open outcry herself. And tell Stan that she could no longer cope with his nightly arrival home at ten in a Scotch-induced stupor. She could no longer handle the fact that they saw each other for a maximum of two hours a day, during which time Angela often wondered whether Stan could see anything at all. Nor could she take his pathetic attempts at physical affection in bed – which essentially meant a thoroughly sodden Stan trying to wedge open her legs with his knee.

Was it any wonder that she now found him about as appealing as a toxic-waste dump? Of course, back when they first met, Stan was most attentive. Not that he was ever any good at articulating his emotions (what bloke – bar self-obsessed Yanks – really is?). But at least he was in evidence around the house. Granted, that was when he was still low down on the corporate ladder – that marital golden age before he became a top trader; before he was paid 300k in exchange for surrendering twelve hours a day, not to mention any vestiges of a home life. And though Stan drank heavily back then, he didn't seem to be as chronically dependent on the bottle as he was now. Angela wondered just how long he could keep up this self-inflicted alcoholic punishment before his boss found him out. Stan was always going on about how he could handle it, how it didn't affect his judgment, how he'd been able to go into the ring after putting away half a bottle of malt and still play with millions of pounds in coffee contracts. Male bravado, she decided, was all about the ability to get it up and make a lot of money with a hangover.

She knew that, early on in their marriage, she'd coerced him into setting his sights on being one of the big boys on the trading floor. And Stan, who was a reserved kind of guy, not exactly brimming with ambition, responded to her persuasion, and his career soon went into the ascendant. Three hundred k – she loved dropping that little figure whenever she went back to Romford. And yet . . . and yet . . . the money had become the marriage. Its perimeters were defined by that 300k. That was why she'd begun to spend so heavily – because the money was the only true line of verbal exchange still open between them.

Anything she demanded of Stan, she got – a fact which infuriated her, and made her spend more. Where was the fight in the man? He had none, really, when it came to his marriage. Which meant, Angela knew, that Stan would probably never fight to keep her. He didn't know how to fight to keep someone's love. The only fight he knew was the kind of mercantile punch-up he engaged in daily in the trading ring. It drained him of any other will to fight, and sent him home a battered heavyweight, oblivious to the world around him.

'He knows I squander money to get his attention,' Angela told herself. 'He knows I sit here in the morning after the au pair's got the kids off to school wondering how I'm going to fill up my day. All right, I could work, but at what? I've never done anything. A year of temping before Jason arrived. That would look very impressive on a c.v., wouldn't it? Anyway, Stan would really climb the wall if I did do some secretarial work on the side – it would make him feel all inadequate, as if he wasn't earning enough. Maybe I should do it for that reason. Might finally get some response out of him . . . Though I keep expecting him to challenge me about the other thing. I know he knows. But he'll never talk about it. Never.'

'The other thing' was Martin. Martin from Dagenham – aged twenty-three and employed as a bouncer at a West End club (where Angela had met him on one of her frequent evenings out with the two Romford girls she still called friends). He looked like a cross between Jason Donovan and a professional wrestler. A four-star toy boy, with a Hoover for a brain – but easy on the eye and quite a good ride, which was more than Angela could say for Stan at the moment. All right, he was rough trade in a Moss Bros monkey suit, but it filled the time. Just like shopping.

Shopping. It was the diamond necklace which finally ruptured things; the diamond necklace she had wanted for her thirty-fifth birthday, and which Stan had wearily consented to purchase for her. Not that he was going to make an appearance at the jeweller's to help her pick it out – that was her 'job'. His job was to pull in the 300k to fund such extravagances. At the time Angela thought: 'That's what he really sees me as: a shopper. That's my true role – to be the person who validates his worth by squandering his money. When I spend, his life is justified. Then he knows why he's killing himself in the FOX ring. All the useless things we buy serve as proof that what he does, the punishment he puts himself through, to earn that 300k is worth it. It's fucking sad, if you ask me. So fucking sad that I'm going to buy that necklace to cheer myself up.'

Lagavulin, Laphroaig, Glenmorangie, Cardhu . . . Lagavulin, Laphroaig, Glenmorangie, Cardhu . . .

On the afternoon of Angela's thirty-fifth birthday, Stan sat in his office and sang the names of his favourite malts in his head. He sang them like an ecclesiastical litany; a Gregorian chant in praise of the medicinal benefits of pure Highland water and barley. *Lagavulin, Laphroaig, Glenmorangie, Cardhu* . . . His pals. His ever faithful companions in time of strife. And today, by Jesus, had been one long day of strife. He was still a half-mil down on the cocoa contracts he'd bought last week, and Jack Jasper was getting exceedingly anxious about every position Stan was taking at the moment. He'd even invited him out to lunch today to sound him out on his 'market strategy'; a lunch during which Jasper stuck to Perrier, while Stan threw down three small whiskies and a half-bottle of claret before making fast work of a double Rémy as a *digestif*. That had been a mistake, Stan now realized, recalling that moment when Jasper's eyes turned arctic as he started slurring a word or three. That had been a big mistake.

The phone on his desk was ringing. Stan knew who it was, but he chose not to answer it. Just as he'd chosen not to answer it hours earlier when Fiona, his secretary, came into his office after he'd staggered back from lunch and said that his wife was on the line, needing approval for some necklace she wanted. 'No calls,' Stan had said, the words thick and molasses-like on his tongue. Half an hour later Fiona was back in his office, saying that Angela was on the blower again, wanting to talk to him urgently. 'No calls,' Stan had repeated, pouring himself another dram of malt from the opened bottle on his desk. Fiona adopted what Stan discerned, through his Islay-induced haze, as a pleading tone:

'But your wife says that the necklace is going to go up by a thousand pounds every . . . '

'Tell her I'm in conference,' Stan said, raising his glass. 'With myself.'

This conference lasted for three hours – until Stan finally looked at his watch and saw that it was seven o'clock. Everyone had gone home, including Fiona, who'd kept unsuccessfully begging him to take Angela's calls all afternoon. He had his feet up on his desk, and was deeply engrossed in the interplay of fluorescent light on the amber liquid swilling around his glass. It felt like the first time in weeks . . . no, months . . . that he'd allowed himself some time to think about nothing. To empty his mind of cocoa futures and sugar positions and Jack Jasper's glacial stare and Angela's untouchability and . . .

The phone rang again. Five rings, eight rings, twelve rings. Stan stared at it, thinking about the words to an old Sinatra song, 'Let's face the music and dance'. Was that the bottom line underscoring all marriages – the knowledge that, no matter how hard you tried to avoid it, you always ended up having to pick up the phone? Was that why Stan finally lifted the receiver?

As he had expected, it was Angela, but what caught him off-guard was the odd timbre of her voice. There was something terribly precise, almost news-readerish about it. She informed him that she'd just bought a necklace. A necklace that cost him £6,000. She had only been planning to spend £2,000, but when she called to talk the matter over with him, his secretary had informed her that he was not taking any calls. Even from his wife. She told Fiona to let Stan know that she was planning to remain in the jeweller's until she got through to him. And for every half-hour he refused to speak to her, she was going to raise the price of the necklace by £500.

'That was four hours ago,' Angela said. 'So the necklace you're going to buy me is now going to cost you four thousand more than it would have if you'd been good enough to speak to me.' She paused for effect. 'Now, what do you think of that?'

There was a silence. A real Grand Canyon of a silence as Stan thought of a reply. But all he could say was . . . 'Nothing.'

The line went dead. Let's face the music and dance? Somehow that song seemed a little inappropriate now. So Stan switched tunes: *Lagavulin, Laphroaig, Glenmorangie, Cardhu* . . .

★   ★   ★

187

Was this the thirtieth or thirty-first cigarette of the day? Angela had lost count. Just as she had lost count of the number of carats in the necklace laid out in front of her. A necklace she now loathed, and knew she'd never wear. But that wasn't going to stop her from writing a £6,000 cheque for it right now. That would teach that bastard a lesson. Show him he can't ignore me.

Cheap melodrama, cheap melodrama. The fact was, Stan wouldn't give a shit about the cheque – a realization that made her hand shake slightly as she began to write out in words, 'S-i-x t-h-o-u . . . .' She could feel the jeweller's eyes register her little tremor, then turn away.

'It was very good of you to stay open so late for me,' she said, trying to fill the silence.

'Our pleasure, madam,' the jeweller said with crisp impersonality. 'How hoity-toity,' she thought. 'England – land of the inscrutably arrogant. A nation of Chinese waiters. I know what he's thinking – that I'm some common *nouveau riche* bitch, putting the thumbscrews on my bloke. Not that he'd dream of even hinting that's what he thinks of me. Oh no – it's all "Yes, madam" and "Of course, madam." Everyone yes's me – Stan especially. Look at that bloody necklace. Why am I buying it? Why does Stan have nothing to say to me? What do I have to do to get his attention?'

She suddenly had a grim idea.

Not one . . . not two . . . but three taxi drivers had refused Stan's custom, once they'd got a whiff of his condition.

'Humiliating stuff,' he later told me. 'Especially when they said they didn't want me doing a Technicolor yawn on their back seat. Not that there was much chance of that, since I'd already spewed in the alley behind my office . . .

'Finally I had to bribe this mini-cab geezer to get me home. Fresh in from Sierra Leone this bloke was, and under the impression that Little Venice was near Dorking. Took two bloody hours, though I don't remember much since I must've been asleep for most of it. And then, when this jungle bunny finally figures out where my front door is, he hits me for twenty quid for the pleasure of getting lost in his S-reg Skoda. Too gone to argue, though. No fight in me at all . . . '

The house was dark; the house was empty. Stan weaved his way through its shadowy corridors. Operating on auto-pilot, he managed to find his way to his bedroom. No Angela. Just a note on his pillow.

'Now, lemme guess what she's written,' Stan said to himself as he threw his shoes across the room: '"Taken the kids to my sister's for the weekend, 'cause you don't love me any more" . . . or words to that effect. Yawn, yawn. Little Miss Predictable. Little Miss . . . '

Stan's head hit the pillow. He was out for the count.

When he was yanked into consciousness some hours later, Stan felt as if he had permanently checked into the twilight zone. The interior of his skull had evidently been used as a nuclear test site during the course of the night, without his authorization. His state of advanced brain damage wasn't aided by the first image that confronted him – Angela's unopened letter on the neighbouring pillow, challenging him to read it and weep.

Let's face the music and . . . open the fucking letter. He ripped the envelope apart. Inside was a plain white card, on which was written an unsigned three-sentence communiqué:

The kids are at my sister's. I am at the Grand Hotel in Eastbourne. If you don't meet me on the beach in front of the hotel tomorrow morning at nine, the marriage is over.

'Tomorrow' was today. And it was now eleven-thirty.

Stan drove fast, fighting off waves of nausea and ire. Bloody bitch. Typical, so typical. Always has to throw a shape. Always has to pull some attention-grabbing stunt like this one . . .

And yet, there was something about the formal, aloof tone of her letter . . . like the formal, aloof tone of her voice yesterday on the phone . . . that chilled Stan a little.

The road to Eastbourne soon became a blocked artery, threatening to bring on cardiac arrest. Traffic slowed right down to 8 mph, and Stan's stomach started doing cartwheels. He caught a momentary glance of himself in the rear-view mirror and wished he hadn't. Shellshocked eyes highlighted by a pair of dark crescent moons between them; a patchy mosaic of stubble adorning his face; hair that looked as if it had been combed with an egg-beater . . . and to top off this Early Derelict image, he was still dressed in the suit that he'd slept in. I look like a walking calamity. I am a walking calamity.

An hour slipped away, followed by another. Stan didn't see the Eastbourne seafront until sometime after two. Dumping the Jag on the first available double yellow line, he did a short sprint to the reception desk of the Grand Hotel. The concierge gave him the once-over and was evidently unimpressed by what he saw. But he did supply him with the information that he'd just missed Angela. She'd gone out around nine this morning, returned at eleven, asking if there were any messages for her, and had left about ten minutes ago.

Stan was out of the door immediately, breaking into a run, dodging traffic on the seafront road before feeling the gritty pebbles of the beach cascade down the sides of his black brogues. He scanned the long grey coastline, but there was no sign of her. He began cantering along the water's edge, vaguely conscious of the stares he was receiving from passers-by. As he ran, he knew what he was going to have to do when he finally found Angela. He was going to have to plead. He was going to have to admit the error of his ways, and make all those boring male promises about spending more time with her and the kids. He was going to have to tell her she was the most important thing in his life and . . .

Gotcha! He saw her, fifty yards ahead of him. He called out

her name, and she turned round and instantly raised her hand in his direction. But what he thought was a gesture of greeting turned out to be Angela adopting the pose of a traffic cop and signalling him to stop.

'You want to talk to me, you can talk to my solicitor,' she shouted.

'Are you crazy?' Stan roared back. He lurched forward, not noticing the unoccupied deckchair that blocked his path, and over which he tumbled, crash-landing into the low-tide sand. A crowd of concerned citizens gathered, staring down at this dishevelled tramp in an £800 suit and making concerned noises about his welfare.

'I'm fine,' Stan said, scrutinizing their faces, hoping to see Angela amongst them. But she wasn't there. He was helped to his feet, but didn't bother to conduct another close visual sweep of the beach, because he knew she was gone. All he could see in the distance was sand. Snapping his eyes shut, he saw sand again. The sand of the desert. That pure white boundless canvas. He was back on his chopper, thundering through the void – only this time, he was stunned by how barren it all was; how stark and inexpressive a void can be. He was finally cruising towards nothing. Finally travelling on a road to nowhere.

A week after that scene on the beach, Stan and Angela agreed to separate.

A month after that scene on the beach, Stan found himself out of a job – a victim, he was told, of profit downturn and pervading economic cheerlessness (though it was also strongly hinted that he might want to get his involvement with malt whisky sorted out before seeking another position in commodities trading).

Six months after that scene on the beach, Stan was still out of work, and could no longer afford the flat he was renting in Butler's Wharf. So he moved back to his mum's house in Stepney.

Nine months after that scene on the beach, Stan and Angela sat down with each other for a frank exchange of views — their first semblance of a proper conversation since separating. At the end of this discussion, two points of consensus were reached. One: Stan would not fight Angela's petition for divorce. Two: the house in Little Venice would go on the market pronto, as the building society's letters about the eight months of mortgage arrears were getting increasingly threatening, and it was only a matter of time before repossession proceedings were instituted against them.

Twelve months after that scene on the beach, the house was sold for £297,000 – £43,000 less than they'd paid for it at the height of the property boom in 1987. After paying off the £20,000 overdraft, and another £7,000 in assorted gold card debts, they were left with just about enough to cover the deposit on a semi in Walthamstow for Angela and the kids.

Fifteen months after that scene on the beach, Angela had become one of those brightly painted women who occupy the ground floor perfume counters of every big department store, and work very hard at maintaining a cheerful public countenance amidst the scents and the scruffing lotions. 'It's a job,' she said when asked about her new employment. 'It pays some bills; it fills the time.'

Stan, meanwhile, sat atop a three-foot stack of newspapers in his new studio flat near Wapping and told me he'd yet to return to the FOX ring, but had been saved from impending destitution by an old client who'd taken him on as a part-time commodities consultant.

'The bloke is paying me two grand a month, which is less than a tenth of what I used to make. Still, it is dosh – and it does mean that I can meet my payments for the kids and also afford the £120 a week for this place – 'cause, much as I love my mum, nine months at home with her in Stepney nearly drove me back to the single malt.'

'You're off the drink?' I asked.

'Almost a year now.'

'You miss it?'

'Only when I'm awake. Still, no booze, no money, and a one-room flat probably means I'm a real nineties man, living the simple life and all that rubbish.

'But y'know what really gets me? The fact that, when I think back to the eighties now, it all seems like it took place last century . . . or was some sort of dream.'

'A good dream or a bad dream?' I asked.

Stan Gould thought that one over for a moment.

'An expensive dream,' he finally said.

Nowadays, when people in London talk about the eighties and its profligate ethic, they tend to adopt a quasi-historical tone – as if it was a dead age, long past memory.

Of course, we like to benchmark history in decades. The sixties are forever labelled a free-wheeling era, even though the first half of the decade was steeped in the chilly conformism of the previous ten years. Similarly, the eighties will always be classified as Greed Unlimited, despite the fact that the avaricious Bang didn't become Big until 1985. And now, in the early years of the nineties, we are told that this is the dawning of the Age of Collective Concern, a time when we will cast off our synthetic status-obsessions and settle down to lives of additive-free wholefoods and environmental awareness. Spiritual concerns will dominate our day-to-day existence. Forget about climbing the corporate *cursus honorem*. Forget about disembowelling the opposition. Forget about driving cars emblazoned with the letters GTi. The pursuit of money will now be conducted in an unabrasive, caring manner, with heavy emphasis on the social responsibility of having big bucks.

After a year of weaving in and out of assorted bourses around the globe, all this talk about the new, 'caring' ethos of the nineties struck me as deeply spurious. Especially since I had returned to a London awash in financial discontent. The recession was in full gloomy swing, City layoffs had become commonplace, and every still-active dealer sang a song along the lines of 'Baby, it's cold out there'. Of course, the top boys and girls in the dealing rooms were still paid serious money, but for many who had drifted into the marketplace over the last ten years (when it had often appeared that just about anybody could get a job as a trader), the party was well and truly over. Who could worry about being a sensitive, humane financier at a time when one's very professional survival on the market floor was so uncertain?

Louise Yew could.

She was thinking about buying dollars early in 1985, so she looked to the sky. What the sky told her was worrying. Mercury was going into retrograde around the middle of March, which meant that serious change was on the horizon. Warning bells immediately went off in her head, and she decided to buy sterling instead. It was a shrewd move. On 17 March the Ohio Savings and Loan Company collapsed, triggering a bad case of the jitters in the world money markets. The American dollar – which had been at near-parity with sterling – hit the skids. And during that month Louise Yew made a neat little profit simply by gauging that Mercury in retrograde meant that it was the right moment to gamble on the resurgent strength of the British pound.

Louise Yew always looks to the sky when plotting her long-term financial strategy as an independent foreign exchange and commodities broker. Back in early 1989, for example, the fact that Saturn was in Capricorn convinced her to buy gold: the presence of that planet in such an earth-orientated sign indicated that it was a good time to back any commodity extracted from terra firma. Similarly, Saturn's arrival in Aquarius after 6 February 1991 was interpreted by Louise to mean that the Gulf War was speeding towards a conclusion, since Aquarius – as any refugee from the 1960s well remembers – is the sign of peace. The convergence of a peace and an earth sign also hinted that social-orientated investments might be a good bet, so she heavily backed a few medical and bio-technological stocks – all of which turned out to be what she calls 'superior profit performers'. Louise Yew figured that she netted a 150 per cent return on that investment – which just goes to show that there's money to be made when Saturn meets Aquarius in the heavens above.

'Playing the markets is a crap shoot,' Louise Yew said. 'That's why everyone who gambles on the exchanges wants to find some sort of indicator which will shorten their odds. The planets have become my racing form; my bookie's sheet.'

Louise Yew is no crank. Nor is she some arcane fortune teller who reads tea-leaves in a low-rent storefront. She is an athletically primed woman in her early forties who exudes high-octane drive and efficiency. When we met at her home in Belgravia she told me she could only spare forty-five minutes, as she wanted to get back to her computer screens in time to check out the afternoon's principal *divertissement* – the opening flurry of activity from the New York Stock Exchange.

Her home verged on the palatial. When I showed up at her front door, I assumed that she and her husband occupied only a floor of this white Regency mansion – one of those formidable buildings off Eaton Square which usually house mid-range foreign consulates or Arabian Gulf trade missions. But Louise Yew owned the entire five-floor establishment. After greeting me, she escorted me up a cascading marble staircase into a formal sitting room that was worthy of Versailles. At this point, the thought struck me: Louise Yew was rich. Seriously rich. As I later discovered, her personal wealth exceeded the GNP of Burundi. She had homes in five cities. She used Concorde the way I used the District Line. And she had this habit of saying things like, 'When I was talking with Henry . . . ' or 'François really is a man of immense charm' – and it took me a minute or two to realize that she was talking about a certain Dr Kissinger and a certain M. Mitterrand.

In short, she was one of those individuals who exist in the upper echelons inhabited by global statesmen and global financiers – a realm which has a very direct bearing on the way the world goes round.

She was also someone who used astrology to plot her every business move. Ask her how she picked up the habit of looking to the sky, and she'll tell you that astrology has always been part of her life; that her father – a Singaporean entrepreneur – used charts to predict economic trends and forecast his investment strategy.

'My father may have employed the planets as a profit indicator,' she says, 'but he was also a great believer in the whole notion of karma in business – the idea that whatever you do comes back to you. So, when it came to doing a deal, he always preached the philosophy that the deal must be fair to all parties. Otherwise, it creates a bad faith and a bad energy which will return to harm you, because energy is a cyclical force.

'Now, I know all this talk about the karma of dealmaking may sound ludicrous. But I'll tell you this – in America, where the prevailing business ethic is "let's flatten the competition", the vast majority of entrepreneurs have tremendously erratic careers, because of all the bad energy they generate through their ruthlessness. But in Chinese or Indian societies – where the whole idea of karma (or the Tao) is an inbuilt part of the culture itself – entrepreneurs tend to have far more stable business lives, with few of the big ups and downs that you'd associate with the Donald Trumps or the Michael Milkens of this world. And the reason is simple: good karma makes for good business.'

Good karma . . . good business? For anyone who wheeled and dealed amidst the survival-of-the-fittest ethos of the 1980s, the idea of blowing away the opposition and then worrying about the cyclical effects of such 'bad energy' must seem downright ludicrous. Just as the whole notion of backing bio-technological stocks simply because Saturn happens to be in Aquarius smacks of stupidity *sans frontières*. All this talk of astrological projection and energy forces gives off a strong whiff of New Agedom. And the New Age has become a sort of counter-culture for a small, but ever-increasing sector of upwardly mobile professionals: a realm where futures traders carry magic crystals on their person while screaming their lungs out in the ninety-day bank bills pit; where advertising executives tell their secretaries, 'No calls for the next half-hour – I'm going to be rebirthing'; and where a certified public accountant will corner you at a party and inform you that, ever since he started taking 'Conscious Living' courses, he's been constantly blissed out.

Outside of talking about your personal relationship with Jesus Christ, probably the surest way to scupper the conversational flow of a dinner party is to inform the table that you've discovered healing energy through the Tao, or the therapeutic benefits of psychic surgery.

In many ways, the ridicule such pronouncements attract is understandable. Thanks to Shirley MacLaine telling the world how she channelled into the spirit of a Stone Age warrior, and David Icke's revelation that disembodied teachers 'from the other plane' have been engaging him in conversation, New Agedom generally has a cosmic freak show reputation. Like born-again Christians, converts to this psychic jumble-sale often display all the tell-tale signs of zealotry. Exponents of Christian fundamentalism and the New Age share a belief that their respective doctrines allow an individual to remake his life – to wipe the spiritual slate clean and reinvent himself anew. The idea of finding a panacea to all of life's conundrums is at the heart of both born-again Christianity and New Agedom. No wonder monomaniacal converts to either doctrine behave as if they have hit upon the only spiritual credo by which to cope with the uncertainties of temporal existence.

And yet, despite all its apparent slick faddishness, a growing number of heavyweight financial honchos in London appeared to be using New Age techniques as a viable business tool, a means to a lucrative end.

'The market really does have a cosmic underside,' Louise

Yew said, 'in the sense that it all comes down to forces beyond us. I truly believe that you can use astrological prediction as a means of turning those forces to your advantage. Just as I also believe that one of the reasons why there has been such a nasty fallout from the 1980s is because so much of the dealmaking at that time was done in bad faith. And, like any energy, bad faith is cyclical – which means that, once you deal it out, it inevitably comes back to get you.'

I said: 'So the nineties will be about good faith in finance?'

'The nineties will still be about getting rich,' Louise Yew said. 'Only now, people will try to become rich in a much nicer, earth plane sort of way.'

Shelley von Strunckel was Louise Yew's astrologer.

'A lot of people like Louise come to me to see what I can predict through the stars. However, to me, prediction is all about trying to get a sense of the world you're going to be dealing with. A good, business-oriented astrologer can say to a client, "Now, I think the climate we're in at the moment will go on for the next six months, but this planet appearing on the horizon represents a definite shift." In other words, an astrological chart can be used as an analytical tool, and I have clients who ask me to use the chart as a means of examining the strengths and weaknesses of their businesses.'

Shelley von Strunckel was an American; a Los Angeleno born with the klieg-lamps of Hollywood shining brightly in her eyes. But to meet her in her Chelsea consulting rooms was to encounter a formidable, rigorously intelligent woman in her early forties who had evidently long parted company with the glitz of her native Beverly Hills. Her husband was a barrister; her interior décor was tasteful Edwardian; her list of clients was gilt-edged.

'Besides my clients who want a forecast on the future, there's a whole different sort of individual – also of the high-achieving persuasion – who uses astrology and New Age techniques for confronting certain personal issues or problems. In this sense,

I can function very much like a shrink. Only whereas a shrink learns about an individual through trained listening, I use an astrological chart to slice into that person's psyche; to take their internal blood pressure.'

By using a map of the heavens based on the date, time and place of her client's birth, Shelley von Strunckel compiles a character profile which essentially points up the conflicts at work within that person's psyche.

'People come to me for an overview of themselves. If they're interested in getting to grips with, say, their hypertension, I can suggest certain techniques – like transcendental meditation – which will not only reduce stress, but will help them make the most of their capabilities. But whereas a lot of New Age charlatans promise their clients that they can remedy life's ills, what I emphasize is the fact that these techniques are merely tools which can help you negotiate your destiny. Do you know that Biblical line, "A time for every purpose under heaven"? Well, as far as I'm concerned, character is destiny – but what I try to help an individual assess is when a time is opportune to pursue something. Because, you see, the core to New Age thinking is the whole idea of self-determination. At its best, New Age thought essentially offers a blend of the rational and the magical, which helps you understand, transcend or take control of some aspect of your life.'

It's no surprise to Shelley von Strunckel that so many financiers are beginning to be referred to her, for she is fully convinced that the dawn of the 'spiritual businessman' is nigh.

'When I talk about a "spiritual businessman", I'm not referring to some holier-than-thou guy who attends prayer breakfasts, or who walks around looking ethereal. What I'm talking about is someone who sees cause-and-effect in business as a combination of recognizing outer trends and inner motivations, and who wants to look within himself in order to enhance his capacity for success. What I offer financiers is entry-level spirituality.'

* * *

I met Anthony Cummings at his club in Pall Mall. From the moment he crisply asked a waiter to get us a couple of large Scotches, I knew there was no way anyone would ever call him a spiritual businessman. He certainly didn't look the celestial part; on the contrary, his penchant for Davidoff cigars and Jermyn Street tailoring – coupled with a richly plummy voice and a patrician demeanour which oozed gravitas – all hinted that I was in the presence of an entrepreneurial heavyweight.

'I'm a very black-and-white sort of chap,' he said, igniting a large Havana special. 'And when it comes to business, I'm exceedingly down-to-earth. So I was terribly sceptical when I first had my chart read by Shelley, and when I also asked her to read the charts of several people I was about to employ at the time. But she turned out to be deadly accurate when it came to assessing their characters. So, when I was about to commence some complex negotiations regarding a company I was about to take over, I had her assess the personalities of the men I'd be wrangling with over the deal. And, once again, she was spot on. So spot on, in fact, that I was able to avoid getting screwed. I was a convert to astrological prediction from that moment on. Not that I understand a damn thing about how it all works.'

Anthony Cummings. Bond merchant. Owner of five companies. Investor in West End musicals. Fully paid-up member of the squirearchy . . . and advocate of good karma in business? Not exactly. But, like many a magnate who has been referred to Shelley (or other astrological consultants), he'd discovered that keeping an eye on the sky could be a remunerative preoccupation.

'Like I said, I was completely dubious about the uses of astrology before I met Shelley – and I must say that I'll probably never be fully convinced by it all. But having said that, the advice she's given me about broadening my business base has, by and large, paid off. As far as I'm concerned, a visit to my astrologer is as much a part of my business life as a visit to my tax consultant or my solicitor – though I really wouldn't admit that too loudly in public.'

Andrew Merchant openly admitted that he visits an astrologer regularly. He also freely admitted to being 'a Type A control-oriented entrepreneur' who used to think he could run his personal life the way he ran his business. But his life had come asunder in the past eighteen months, and he'd been using New Age techniques to try to put it back together again – which explains, in part, why he was so freely admitting his personal defects at the moment.

I met Andrew in a lounge at Heathrow Airport. It was his choice of venue, as he didn't have time to see me in his office ('The next appointment window I have free is in five weeks' time'), but he thought he might be able to give me a thirty-minute drink window before he caught the last flight of the day to New York.

Andrew talked a great deal about windows. And about risk arbitrage. And about the virtues of phatic language in the marketplace. He was a walking lexicon of techno-speak and buzz-words. And he organized his life with the mathematical precision of a time-and-motion analyst. Even at a first meeting, in the synthetic confines of an airport bar, he was clearly a man who had spent much of his adult life in the pursuit of personal perfection. At the age of forty, there wasn't a hint of corpulence on his torso. He had the sort of sculpted cheekbones which creative directors favour for selling after-shave. His clothes were by Cerutti, his luggage by Coach. He was an image-conscious, attention-to-details type who evidently travelled through life on high-octane. And he had recently suffered a sequence of major emotional car crashes.

'The last eighteen months were a complete nightmare,' he said. 'My marriage broke up, my brother died, my financial investment business went sour, and a relationship I got into after I left my wife also came apart. It was like living in the personal equivalent of Beirut. But even though it was the worst

201

year of my life, the fact that it was so bloody awful made me reassess and take stock of things.'

Taking stock of things for Andrew meant a couple of sessions with a shrink. But, as someone who demands instant results, the idea of three years on the couch in the company of a silent Freudian didn't exactly thrill him. So he went for an astrological reading, and found that what the consultant saw in his chart was an exceedingly accurate reflection of the heavy weather that was swamping his psyche. When the consultant suggested that transcendental meditation might enable him to get a better grip on things, he put aside his preconceptions and signed up for a course of instruction.

'What I learned about TM was this: at heart, it all comes down to sitting alone in a room by yourself for twenty minutes twice a day and basically relaxing your mind and body. It's a totally passive activity – which, for a thoroughly impatient human being like me, was hard to get used to. TM has helped me to slow down a little bit, and maybe to listen a little more carefully to what other people are saying. I mean, even though my business went through the shits in 1990, I've still made enough money over the years not to have to work again – which is not a bad position to be in. TM (and now yoga, which I've also taken up) has taught me that I don't have to keep score in life any more. And it finally made me address the question: am I going to control my life, or is my life going to control me?'

Listening to Andrew talk, I was reminded of the way recent converts to born-again Christianity wax lyrical about their newly-found spiritual uplift. When I raised this point with him, he was quick off the mark, saying:

'Let me tell you the big difference between a born-again Christian and a New Ager. The born-again says, "I'm serving Him," whereas the New Ager says, "I'm serving Me." And that's why so many business guys I know are going New Age – because they realize it's all about personal payoff. Success without the stress.'

Did Andrew Merchant represent the stress-managed, psychically aware financier of the future? Or was he simply one of the lucky few who had survived the eighties with his killing intact and could now afford the luxury of alternative thoughts about the quest for money? Just as I was beginning to wonder whether he did exemplify a new wave of spiritual dealmaker, he told a joke. A joke which let it be known that, though the decade of cupidity was dead, it was still business as usual when it came to chasing mammon. Only now, the game was going to be played by a kinder and gentler set of rules.

'Ever heard the one about the young bull and the old bull standing on top of a hill, looking down on a field full of cows? The young bull turns to the old bull and says, "Let's run down there and screw us a couple of cows." And the old bull replies: "No – let's *walk* down there and screw them all."

'That, my friend, is the nineties way of doing business.'

Then he excused himself and moved off in the direction of the Club Class check-in counter. Walking, not running.

Stephen White also believed in walking, not running.

'You know what my business philosophy is? Steady, steady, steady. Don't act the Flash Harry. Don't try to be Number One when it comes to making money. Just maintain your profit performance and keep your head down. That's the whole key to staying alive in the City right now.'

Stephen White certainly looked the steady type. He was Mr Grey Worsted personified – a balding thirty-five-year-old man in a nondescript suit who stared out at the world from behind a pair of plain black spectacles. His white shirt was heavily starched; his tie a funereal print. When he spoke, his voice always maintained the same uniform, balanced tone. Everything about him exuded restraint and caution. To meet him was to ask yourself how someone could be so calculatingly ordinary.

As I discovered, he cultivated this aura of unobtrusiveness as a form of shield; a way of dodging the problems inherent in calling attention to oneself. He was an options salesman in the City dealing room of a major European bank. Walking on to this trading floor I encountered all the standard-issue pandemonium I had come to associate with a financial market-place – that is, with the exception of the area around Stephen White's desk. It was a small island of apparent sanity amidst the hysteria. While his fellow dealers and salesmen screamed down their phones, Stephen methodically dialled client after client, never raising his voice above a normal conversational tone. When I later asked him over an after-work drink how he avoided being drawn into the frenzied fray of the dealing floor, he mentioned his philosophy of business yet again:

'Steady, steady, steady.'

If you can keep your head when all about you are losing theirs . . . then you might just be a City survivor like Stephen White.

'You know what the younger salesmen call me?' he asked. '"The fossil" – because, as far as they're concerned, I've been around on the floor since the Palaeozoic era.'

'Exactly how long have you been there?' I asked.

'Five years.'

'Five years make you a fossil?'

'Believe me, the way things are in the City at the moment, surviving five years on any trading floor probably qualifies you for a place in the Natural History Museum.'

Stephen White quickly scanned the wine bar to make certain no colleague was within earshot of such irreverence. He needn't have worried – it was almost empty.

'If you want to see how the City has changed since the Crash, just look at this place. Two years ago, it was so packed after work you couldn't even find a place to stand. The entire Options Division came in here every night and drank champagne on a company credit card. Now it's almost always empty – because every company I know has cut back on expenses and, anyway, most people in the square mile are keeping a low profile these days. It's the same with restaurants

204

around here. Yesterday I took two of my Japanese clients out to lunch at this rather posh place where you used to have to book a table a week in advance. But yesterday we were the only people there – which, as you can imagine, was a shade embarrassing. Especially since the Japanese like a bit of a crowd around them when they're doing business.

'I guess, when you get right down to it, I'm just happy to have a job. A lot of chaps I know who were real high flyers have crash-landed in a big way. Just last week I had a drink with a mate of mine who was one of the biggest options dealers during the eighties. At the height of the boom, he was easily pulling down £250,000 a year. Every week some other company was trying to seduce him away from us with a big fat offer. And he always used to slag me about being just a mid-level salesman who simply maintained a steady level of business for the company. But once the recession hit, it was the solid plodders like me who kept their jobs, and the Top Guns like him who were out the door. They simply couldn't keep generating the high level of dosh that was needed to match their big salaries. And, you know, he hasn't been able to find work in over two years. The man's just about lost everything.'

I asked Stephen if he had ever been tempted by the financial rewards offered to City high flyers. 'Once,' he said, and explained that his whole career to date has been all about selling somebody something. After he received his degree from Sussex University, he spent four years on the road as a sales rep for a major pharmaceutical concern. When he finally grew tired of all the travel ('after eating one breakfast too many at Little Chef'), he decided to take his sales talents to the City. He was over the moon when he landed a job as a stock salesman in the London office of a big American bank. For Stephen, the real pleasure in selling stocks was assuming the role of storyteller: trying to capture the imagination of a customer by weaving him a tale about the state of a company and what its growth curve might be.

'I was dead keen on the work. So keen that for the seven years I was with the bank I was probably making them around £1 million a year in sales. But then, one January morning in 1986 – in fact, the day after I arrived back at the office from the Christmas holidays – my secretary told me I was wanted in Room 104. When I got there, I was handed a letter by some flunky informing me that I was being made redundant. Guess why I was being given the shove. Head office in New York wanted to streamline the London division, so they decided that their most expensive salesmen would have to go.

'As you can imagine, I was a touch upset by the news – especially since it came only a fortnight after my wife had given birth to our second child. And what I couldn't get over – what I still can't get over – was the way they went after the real big earners in the company. Because, we might have been making them a lot of money, but we were obviously costing them a lot too. Luckily, there was still plenty of work in the City back in '87, so I managed to land this job selling options less than a month after being laid off. But the whole experience taught me a very simple lesson: if you want to keep alive in the financial marketplace, maintain a low profile. Make just enough money for the company to regard you as reasonably cost effective, but never draw too much attention to yourself. Be boring.'

'Do you consider yourself boring?' I asked.

'Exceedingly so. I am your average City man – the same sort of chap who worked here fifty years ago, and will still be working here fifty years from now. I have a reasonably well paid, reasonably satisfying job, I have a wife and two children, a house in Surrey, and a choice between the 18.20 and the 18.50 back from Waterloo. It's what is known as an ordinary life.'

An ordinary life. Many months earlier, in a club near Wall Street, another achromatic financier had told me that he too lived an existence of supreme conventionality. It made me wonder: were the ultimate financial survivors of the eighties the Grey Men of the marketplace; the solid, unostentatious types who have always quietly ensured the continuing existence of every bourse on earth? And didn't they already know something that Andrew Merchant and his New Age ilk were just finding out: manic ambition is ultimately dangerous to your health.

Success without the stress. Was that the secret desire of every man and woman of commerce? But was stress a necessary mechanism for surviving in the realm of finance? If my time amongst the dealers had taught me anything, it was this: the pursuit of money is a traumatizing experience. Yet that trauma isn't really bound up in the trauma of the marketplace. Rather, it stems from the way money has become the way we validate our time on the planet, and try to live up to the expectations of our own society. As I discovered in Casablanca, a financial marketplace is nothing more than a hi-tech souk. Yet – as any shrewd merchant well knows – when a man or woman engages in the act of barter, they are exposed for what they truly are.

'Is that all you learned after twelve months in all those markets?' Stephen White asked me.

'No, I learned one other thing.'

'What was that?'

'Everybody has an 18.50 to catch.'

'Quite right,' he said, and headed out to make his train.